CW01262102

WHITE STAR PUBLISHERS

Texts
Guido Barosio

Editorial coordination
Giulia Gaida
Livio Bourbon

Graphic design
Michela Barbonaglia

Translation
C.T.M., Milan

© 2001 White Star s.p.a.
Via C. Sassone, 22/24
13100 Vercelli, Italy
www.whitestar.it

New updated edition in 2007

All rights reserved. No part of this publication may be reproduced, stored in a retrieval system or transmitted in any form or by any means, electronic, mechanical, photocopying, recording or otherwise, without written permission from the publisher. White Star Publishers® is a registered trademark property of White Star s.p.a.

ISBN 978-88-544-0256-0
Reprints:
1 2 3 4 5 6   11 10 09 08 07

Printed in China

PLACES AND HISTORY

morocco

CONTENTS
INTRODUCTION	PAGE	8
THE GLORY AND BATTLES OF AN AFRICAN EMPIRE	PAGE	20
DUNES, MOUNTAINS AND FORESTS IN THE COUNTRY OF A THOUSAND COLORS	PAGE	46
FROM THE IMPERIAL CITIES TO THE GATEWAY TO THE DESERT	PAGE	74
NOMADS AND RIDERS: SLOW PASSING OF TIME	PAGE	122
INDEX	PAGE	132

1 A detail of the superb gateway to the Royal Palace in Fez. The king has a private residence in each of the Imperial Cities that he uses at least once a year. Only the king and his retinue are allowed to use these palaces which were built in different epochs but all have been restored and recently modernized.

2/7 This engraving from 1860 shows a caravan halted at the gates of Marrakesh. "Ships of the desert" and merchants have always been a popular artistic theme of Morocco.

3/6 The Dadès valley in the southern High Atlas mountains is also known as the "Valley of a thousand Kasbahs." A long series of castles in this area marks an imaginary frontier with the Sahara.

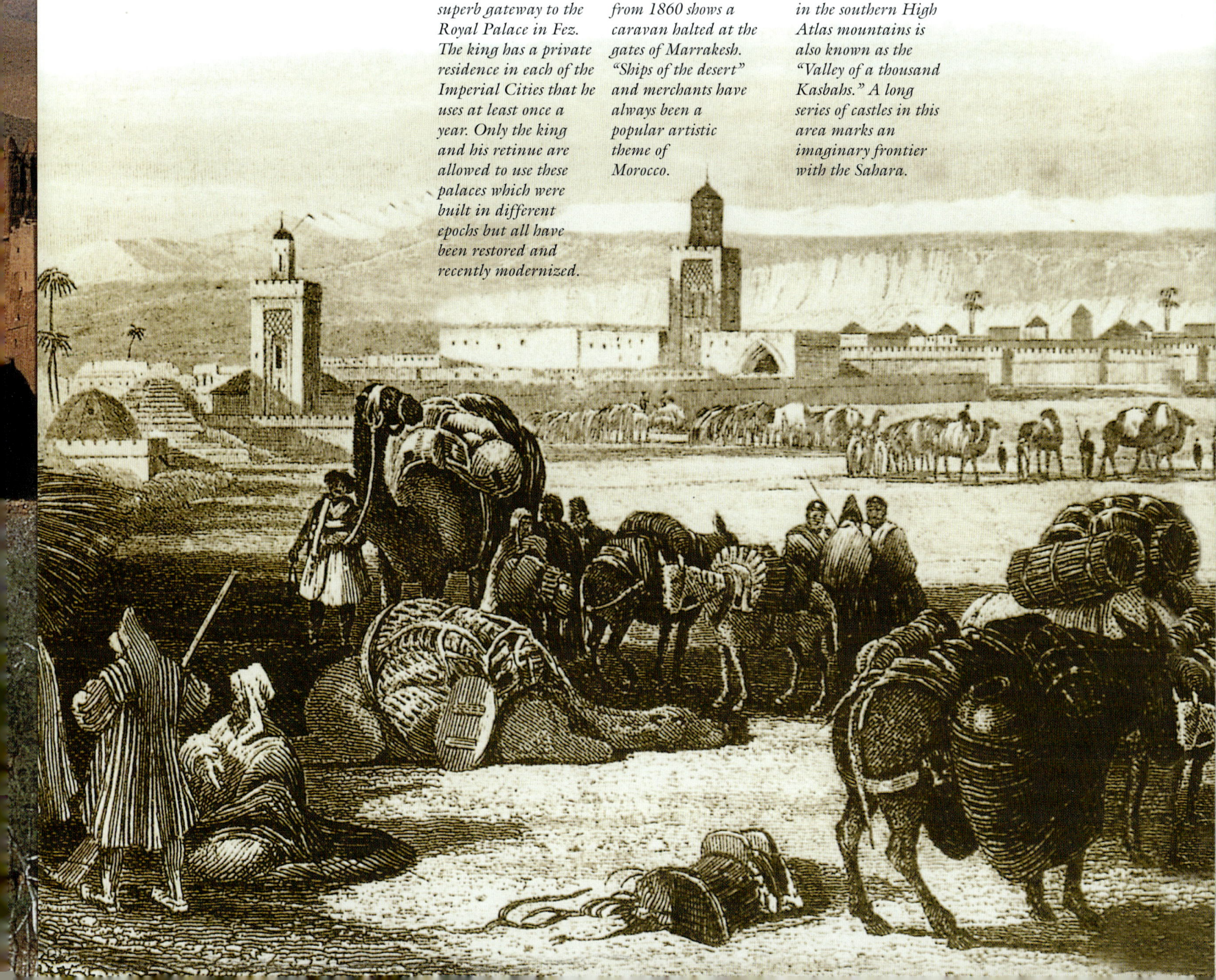

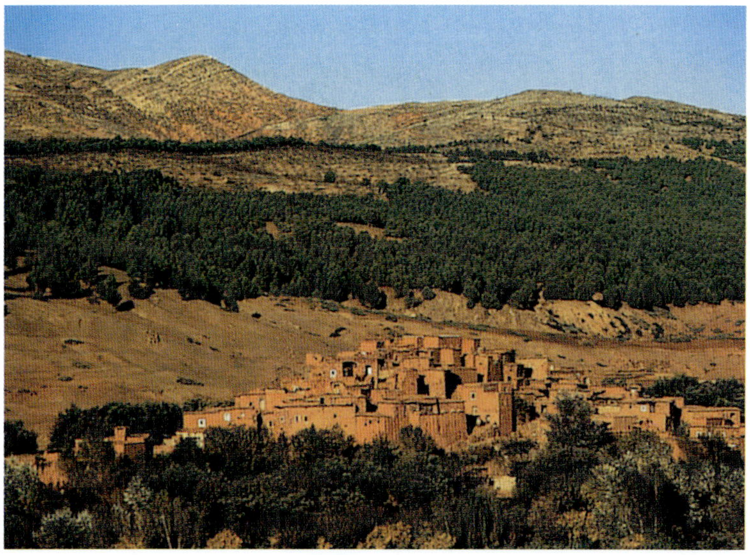

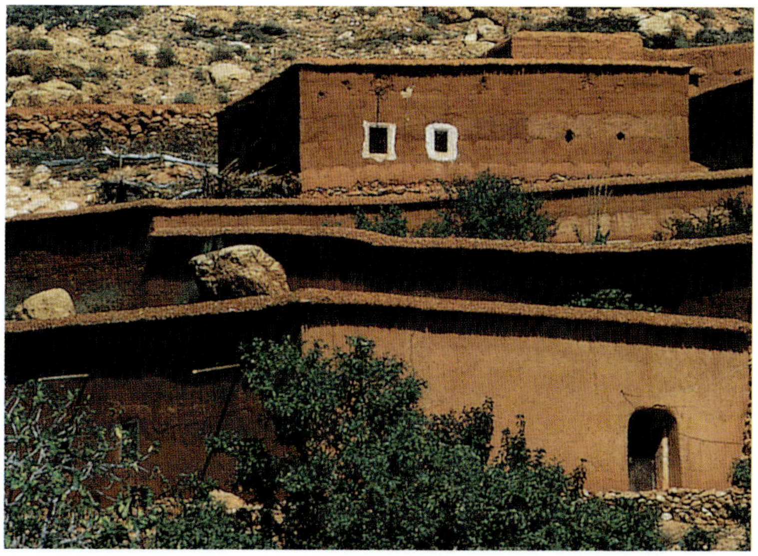

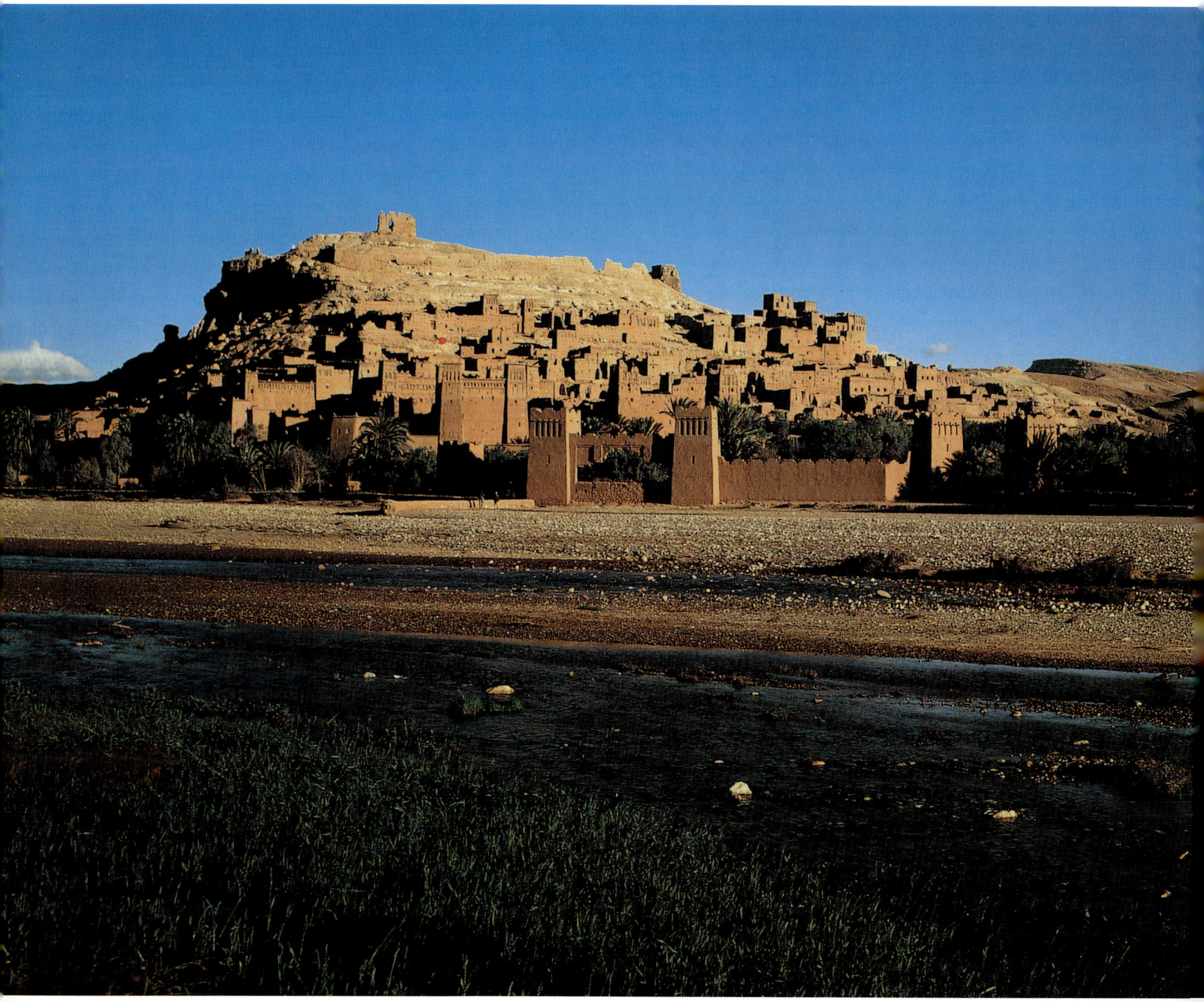

10 top left The green countryside of the Ourika valley lies a few miles from Marrakesh at the foot of the High Atlas; named after its river, the valley is fertile with a mild climate and is now the location of a few tourist facilities.

10 top right Traditional Berber houses in a village in the Valley of the Roses, a few miles from Boumaline. Agriculture and human settlements, often protected by austerely beautiful forts, are made possible by the river Dadès.

10-11 The river Ouarzazate separates the steppes from the city of the same name and the kasbah *of Taourit. Morocco has numerous fortified villages, often protected by tall and solid walls that are a reminder of when powerful local rulers often clashed with imperial power.*

11 top right After the snows melt on the Oukaimeden plateau, extensive meadows similar to European mountain pastures are revealed. Yet, just a few hours journey will take you from this cold setting to the first dunes of the Sahara.

people who were both mystical and mysterious and whose language is still spoken unchanged by a quarter of the country's population. Warriors, animal breeders and sometime plunderers, the Berbers knew how to negotiate with other peoples without compromising themselves. The Phoenicians colonized the coast but hardly touched inland and their influence was essentially commercial and religious. Following the destruction of Carthage and the conquest of Mauritania, Roman settlements began to prosper whose masters were concerned with military control of the coast and good relations with the inhabitants of the interior. The result was a Roman-Berber population in centers like Cotta, Tamuda, Lixus and, above all, Volubilis, the remains of which have survived the ravages of time and are now one of northern Africa's loveliest archaeological sites, but these historical developments had almost no influence on the tribes further inland. They were heavily affected, however, by the Arab invasion and the arrival of Islam which brought a military, social and religious revolution that altered the destiny of the Berbers but which only minimally diluted their ethnic purity. The nomadic and anarchic herders became feared warriors that fought in support of the Islamic religion; they conquered kingdoms and cities but lost them again just as quickly. Dynasties and wars followed hard on one another, igniting the Atlantic and Mediterranean coasts as well as Spain, Portugal and the edges of black Africa.

Strategically located on the divide between two continents, Morocco represented the ideal of a Berber and Islamic empire in a fusion of the region's oldest traditions and the faith based on belief in a single God that was the unifying element among all peoples from the Atlantic to the Indian Ocean. Islam was the lifeblood of a civilization of great refinement that was equally advanced in arts and sciences. Today, the magnificent imperial cities of Morocco still reflect the splendors of a period that brought together Arab traditions with Hispanic and Moorish architecture of unequalled imagination. Generations of architects, craftsmen, slaves and carpenters gave form to the dreams of the caliphs by constructing and decorating glorious palaces, mosques and gardens. Only progressive economic penetration by the French and Spanish combined with a political instability that was perhaps innate in Berber customs brought the system to crisis point. Starting in the 19th century, Morocco progressively lost its liberty and autonomy until it entered the darkest phase of its history but it never completely lost its independence, the only country in the whole of Africa able to make that boast. In 1955, under Mohammed V, the monarchy regained complete control of the situation and today, thanks to the efforts of Hassan II, it seems more solid than ever. Skilled in wriggling out of crises and escaping assassi-

11 bottom right The kasbahs *are forts built centuries ago by local sultans and share certain achitectonical features: high walls and towered houses.*

12 bottom On the boundary of the Sahara in the extreme south of the country, "blue men" live by trading camels and handcrafts. The picture shows a Berber carpet tradesman in the typical clothes of the Tuareg tribes.

12-13 A Berber woman wearing the traditional headcovering and her daughter prepare for a festival. The traditions of this people in the racial mosaic of Morocco are still strong, especially in rural areas.

13 top left Wearing traditional costume, the Berber tribes celebrate the anniversary of the birth of the Prophet. Without abandoning their more ancient traditions and ceremonies, the Berbers embraced Islam when it arrived with the Ummayads.

13 top right The white streets of the well preserved medina in Chechaouen are the oldest part of the city; the life of the people here has only minimally been affected by modern life.

woods of arganias, red junipers and Atlas pistachios, then there is the forest of Mamora, with its 212 square miles of eucalyptuses, acacias and cork oaks. The abundant and widely varying flora enjoys a mild climate where the hot winds of the Sahara are mixed with the temperate, if not cold, winds of Europe. In addition, there are the two coastlines: the Mediterranean, with its ports and commerce, where the mountains fall straight down into the water, and the Atlantic, where the cliffs worried by the ocean waves alternate with huge beaches like those at Agadir.

nation attempts, this king succeeded in maintaining a delicate balance between modernity and tradition by drawing back from voracious capitalism and the religious extremism that has so bloodied neighboring Algeria. Hopes of stability now rest with his heir, Mohammed VI.

The geography of Morocco is as extraordinary as its history is fascinating. The beauty and variety of landscapes take one's breath away. The changeless and inviolable rolling dunes of the desert are only halted by the slopes of the Atlas mountains where the tallest peaks are permanently snow-covered. The harshness of the Atlas range suggests lunar landscapes where man has never set foot and proved ideal for settings for some scenes in the film *Star Wars*. Indeed the whole of the country seems as though it were created specially for film locations and artistic scenery. But where the desert ends and the mountains slope down towards the Mediterranean, the huge open spaces and the wilderness are transformed into an endless gentle countryside. Cedar forests cover 290 square miles, then there are emerald green pastures,

The works of man provide stiff competition for the variety of landscapes. The histories of the ports of Tangiers and Casablanca are replete with traders, adventurers, poets and pirates. Rabat and Meknes are monuments to the solemnity of power and religious faith with the beauty of the *kasbah* and the silence of the necropolises. Fez enchants with the intricacy of its *medina* in which the full range of man's imagination seems to have been transformed into architecture. And finally there is Marrakesh, the most African of Morocco's cities and the gateway to the desert and the heights of the Atlas mountains. In the smoke and clamor of its market, the visitor will find the true soul of Morocco and, should he have lost it, also his own.

There is no reason, then, to be surprised that Morocco has always attracted western culture more than any other North African country. Pierre Loti, Le Clézio, Saint-Exupéry, Paul Bowles, Eugène Dealcroix, Tennessee Williams, Jean Genet, Poul Morand and even Bernardo Bertolucci and Gabriele Salvatores have been influenced, in some cases bewitched, by the smells, the silences, the people and the immense natural beauties of this hugely varied country. Morocco, as it always has been, is a kingdom of the sun kissed by two seas.

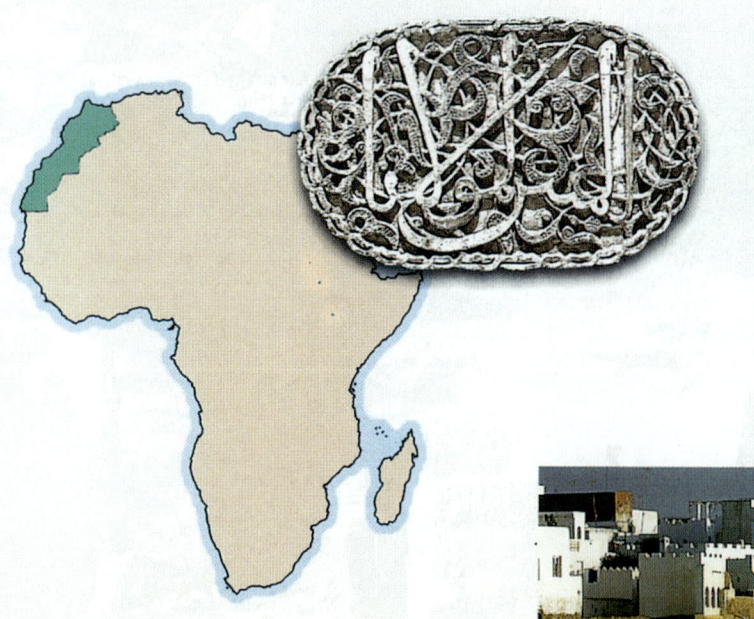

Green palms in the Moroccan Sahara.

The medina and fortifications at Asilah.

Blooming on Oukaimeden plateau.

The kasbah in Ait Arbi in the Dadès valley.

Threshing in a Berber village.

The Rif near Chechaouen.

Spain

Mediterranean Sea

Tangiers · Ceuta
Karache · Tétouan
· Chechaouen
Mamora forest   Rif
Rabat · · Volubilis
· Fez
Casablanca · Meknès
El Jadida · Middle Atlas

The Atlantic Ocean

Essaouira · Marrakesh   High Atlas   · Erfoud
Tizi N'Tichka · Télouet   · Rissani
Djebel Toubkal ▲   Ouarzazate   Dadès
Agadir · Taroudannt   · Zagora   Todra
Sous
Tafraout
Anti Atlas

The Canary Islands

Tarfaya
Draa

Algeria

· Smara

Boujdour

Ad-Dakhla

The western Sahara

Mauritania

16-17 The Dar al-Badi palace was built by Ahmed al-Mansour, the victorious sovereign at the Battle of the Three Kings, but he died before it was completed. Every summer, the site is the location of the largest popular festival.

18-19 The high dunes of Merzouga are continuously shaped by the winds and mark the start of the enormous expanse of sand that spreads for several hundred miles beyond the border into Algeria.

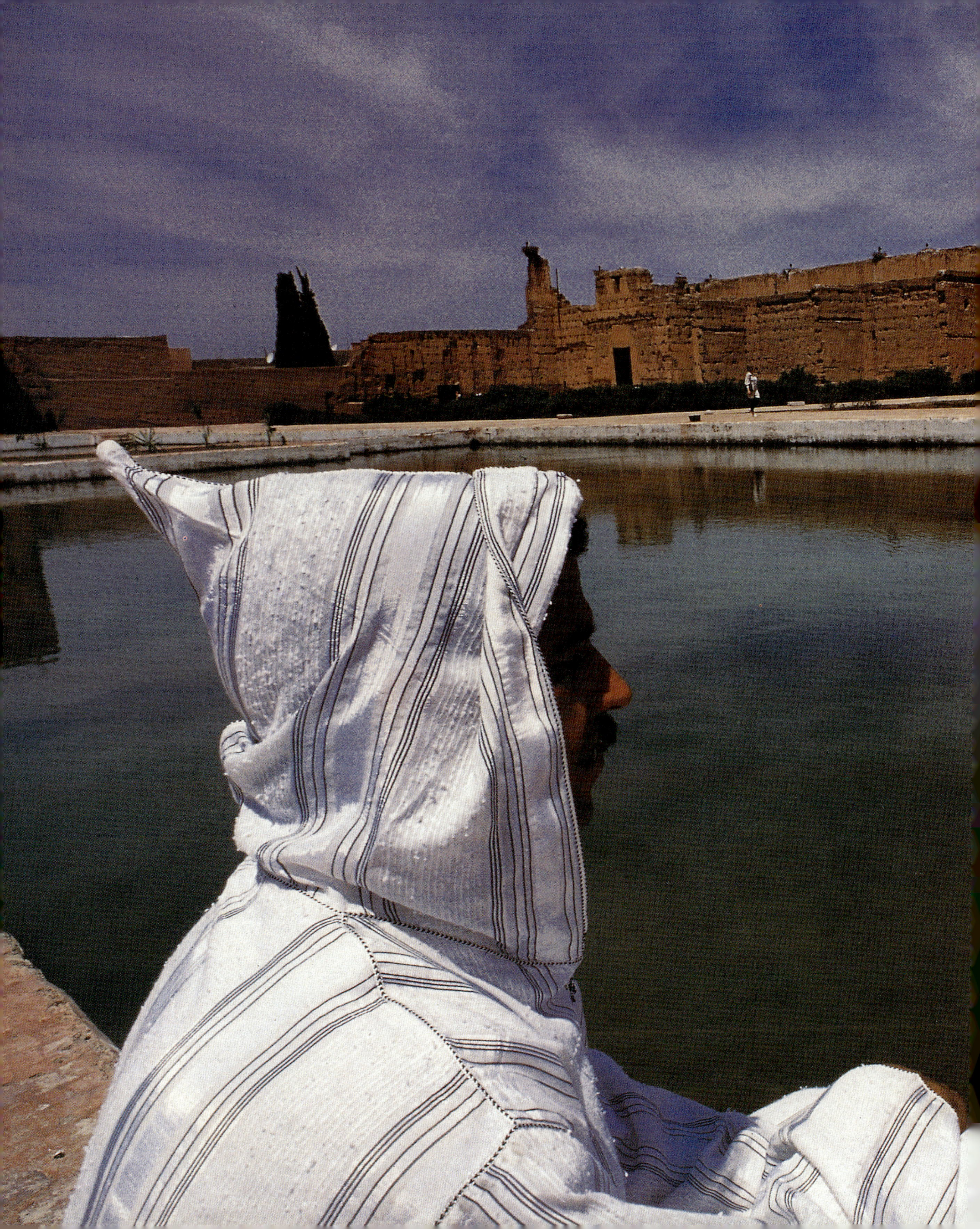

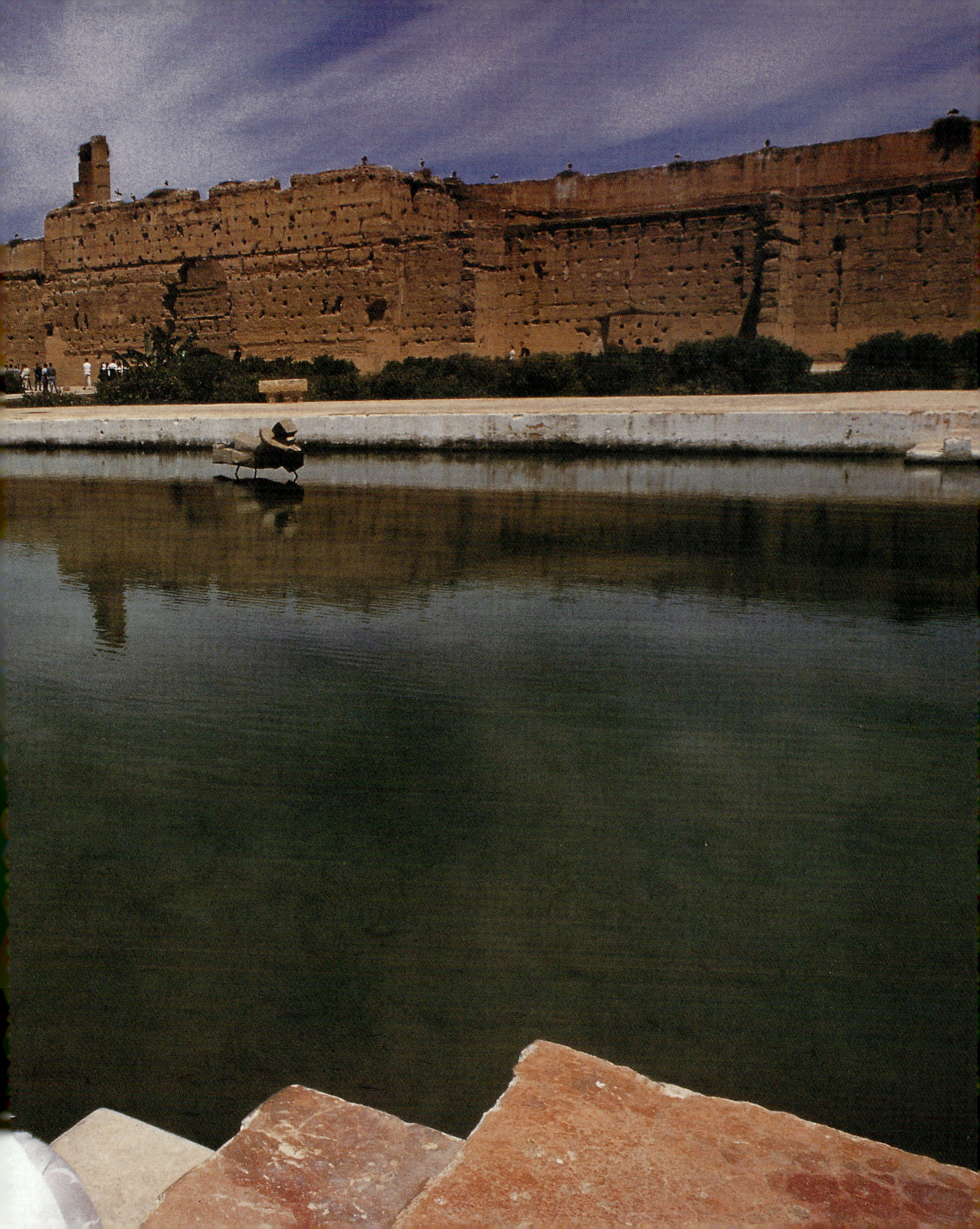

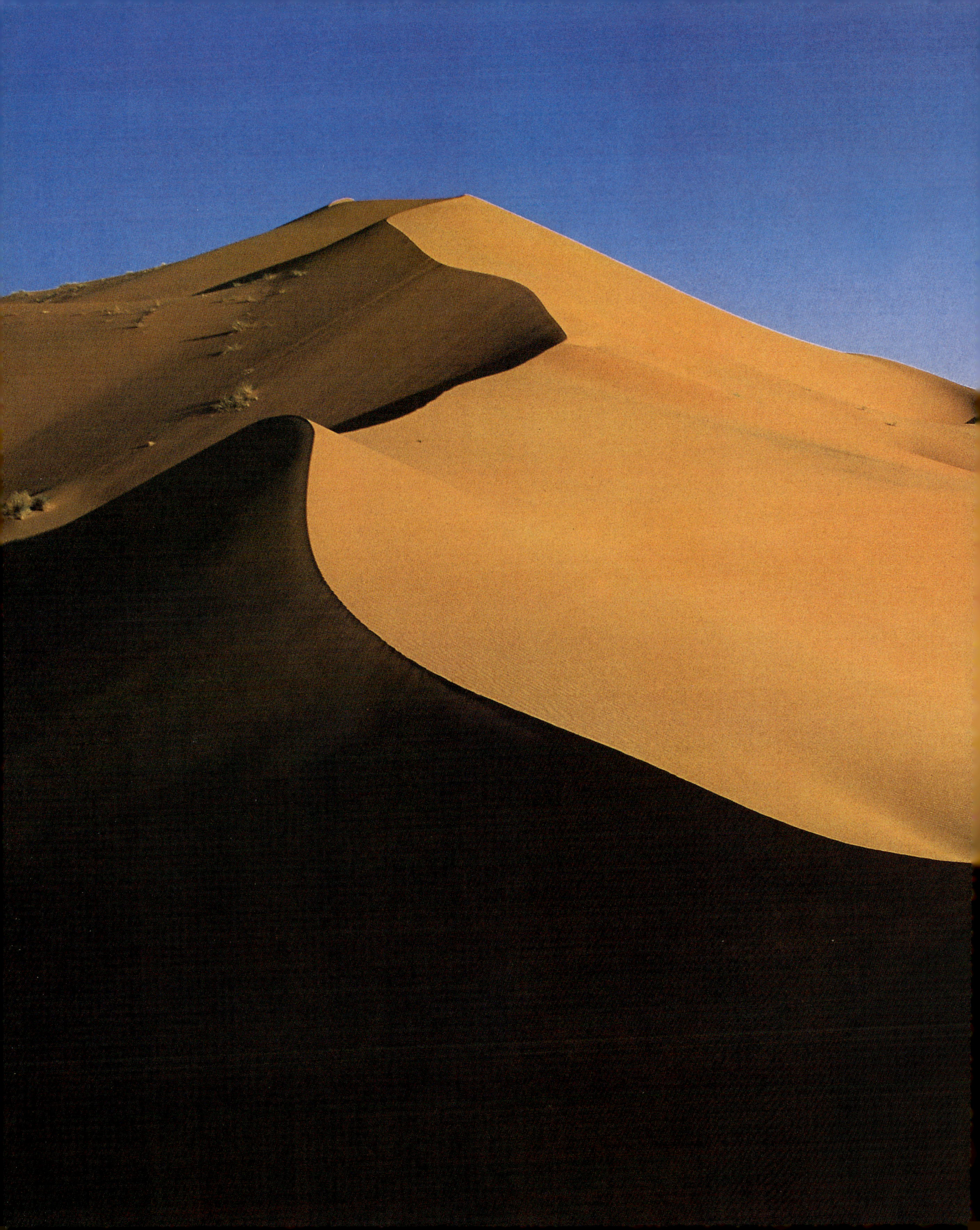

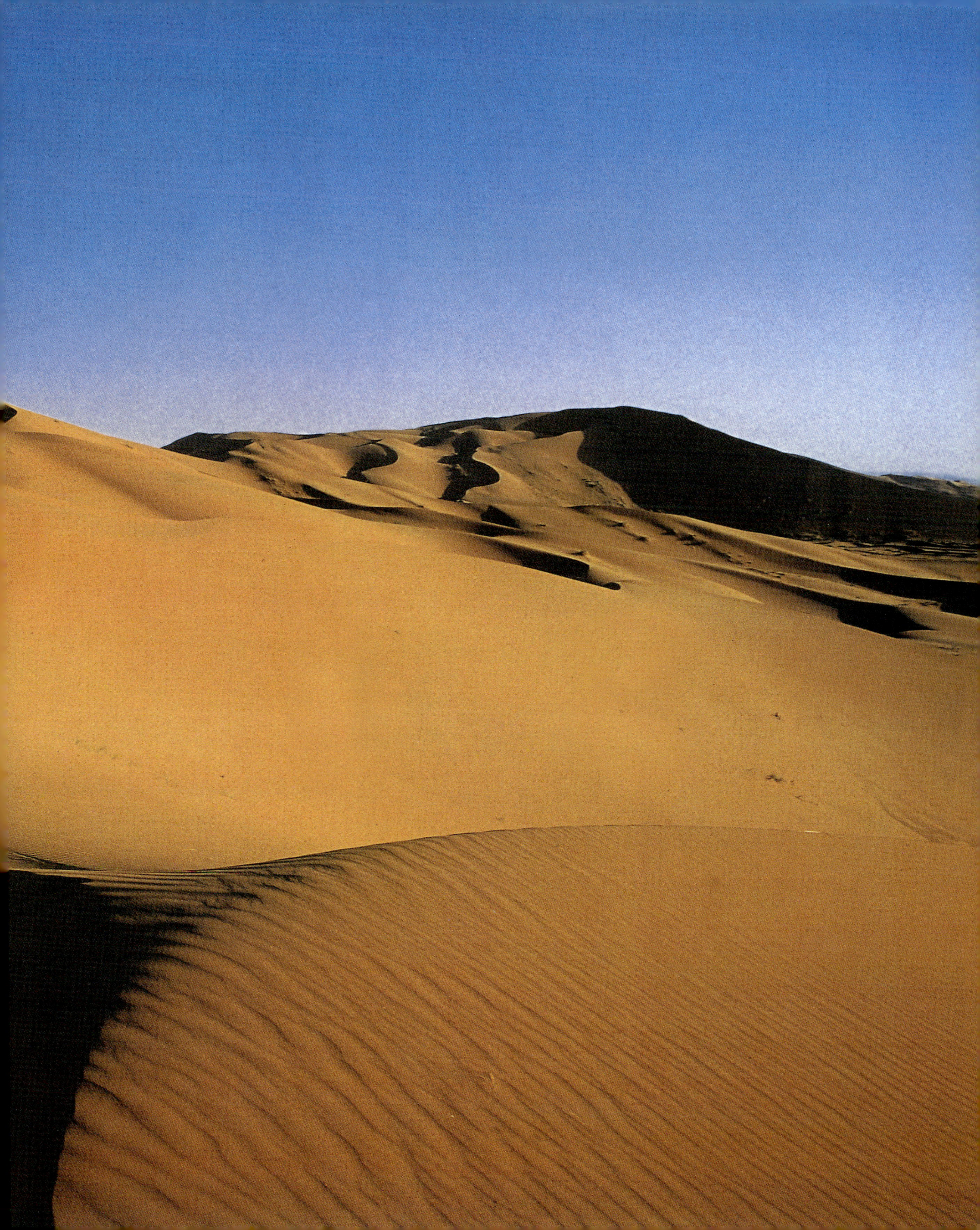

THE GLORY AND BATTLES OF AN AFRICAN EMPIRE

Risky conquests and powerful empires, royal dynasties and pirates, colonizers and nomadic tribes; the history of Morocco has been the result of its geography and its unusual position of "border land" between Africa and Europe, between Islam and the Maghreb. The Mediterranean coast of Morocco faces Spain where Ceuta and Gibraltar almost touch while the Atlantic coast stretches down further than the Tropic of Cancer. Morocco is hemmed in not only by the ocean but by a desert so featureless that it can only be divided on a map by drawing a line to signal where Algeria ends or Mauritania starts. The mountains between the ocean and the desert are divided into the Little, Middle and High Atlas and their many peaks, valleys and gorges are more features of the complex and extreme landscape of Morocco. The result is a country that has never been completely controllable due to the many natural barriers and shelters that create an unlimited number of hiding places and means of escape. The history of Morocco has one running theme: the attempt, many times frustrated, of the more orthodox and organized coastal governments to subdue the interior and the organized anarchy of its Berber tribes, for the Berbers – nomadic warriors and stock-raisers – were restless by nature and rebellious by tradition.

This contrast is still evident today in the geographical names of the territory: the central zone of the country occupied by the administrative powers (the area nearest the coast and the large imperial cities) is known as *Bled al-Makhzen*, "the land of the regime," while the desert and mountain region is called *Bled al-Siba*, the "lawless lands."

Legend recounts that Morocco's history began when the ancestors of the Berber tribes arrived in the country from the mythical continent Atlantis which used to be connected to the current ocean coast. What is certain is that the first hominids were present in Morocco 800,000 years ago. This is proven by archaeological finds made in Casablanca that are unques-

20 These rock inscriptions of hunting scenes practiced by the Berbers, the earliest inhabitants of the Atlas mountains, are seven thousand years old. At the time, much of the desert and rocky territory of Morocco was covered by woods, forests and grasslands.

20-21 This map, dated 1664, was drawn by Athanasius Kircher and shows Atlantis, the legendary land supposedly off the African coast that was swallowed up in a cataclysm. Myth says that Atlantis was the homeland of the Berbers.

tionably the oldest in northern Africa.

In 5000 BC, the Sahara region was still grassland populated by zebra, giraffes, elephants, hippopotamuses and rhinoceroses. Numerous inscriptions found in the High Atlas depict hunting scenes with these animals. Who were these first mysterious inhabitants? The original lords of north-west Africa were certainly Berber (also called Mauritanians) but what is not known is where they came from. If we exclude the enjoyable but unproven hypothesis that they did indeed come from "Atlantis," we are obliged to accept the theory of "ethnic unification" between tribes of different geographic provenance, often distant. This would explain their common language and alphabet and the modern day existence of individuals with fair skin and blue eyes, while others are very dark and appear to have Ethiopian features. These people were to become the restless spirit of Morocco.

They were difficult to control because they were in continual movement, either following their flocks or hunting prey and caravans to plunder, and they had a special and exclusive relationship with the land. The deserts and mountains formed perfect settings for ambushes and hiding places, natural barriers to enemies and safe refuges for herds and camps. Another reason for the survival of the Berbers was their innate willingness to compromise. They became the allies of all the large coastal civilizations but they were never subjected.

There were divisions of responsibilities and areas of influence but there were also intertribal marriages so that the purity of the original peoples was diluted over the centuries to produce mixed civilizations and races. Little remains of the original Berber tribe and their ethnic purity has probably been lost forever but their contribution to the history of Morocco has been a natural restlessness. It is as though the nomad spirit, absorbed by other dominant groups, has taken its revenge by creating instability in the overall order.

22 This cast of a detail of the Trajan Column shows the cavalry of Mauritania. At the time of Carthaginian rule, Mauritania was an independent state inland and only later did it become a Roman protectorate. The cast can be seen in the Museum of Roman Civilization.

The winds of the Sahara and the spirit of its people rendered the great victories of those that came from distant lands - the Phoenicians, Romans, Arabs and French who wanted to create in Morocco the largest kingdom in North Africa – more fragile and provisional.

Morocco's known history began with the presence of the Carthaginians on the coasts of the Mediterranean. The first Phoenician colonies were created in 1100 BC with the names Rusadir (now Melilla) and Links (which later became Lixus). These coastal settlements were founded by great navigators who were unwilling to travel inland but they constituted a solid base for trade and contacts with local tribes. Based on a mixture of agree-

23 left Roman gold coin depicting the Berber prince Juba II found at Volubilis. Juba was appointed by Augustus and reigned from 25 BC-23 AD. Although his state was not a Roman province, he was made to pay regular tributes to Rome.

23 right An elegant bronze figure of Juba II as a young man. The last king of independent Mauritania was an able politician and economist; he increased the production of purple and sent a fleet to explore the Canary Islands.

ments and raids, a forum for exchange and trade useful to the Phoenicians was created; from the interior arrived food for the cities and naval expeditions while in return the nomads were able to purchase manufactured goods. The Phoenician presence lasted until 146 BC when Carthage was destroyed during the Third Punic War. The relationship between the new rulers of the coast and the Berbers began on the same basis as with the Phoenicians - coastal settlements, trading and conveniently separate areas of influence - but the structure of the Roman state and its political vision were much more developed. Consequently, the situation changed during the last fifty years of the century with expansion inland made necessary by continuous incursions by North African marauders in Tunisia which, at that time, was a faithful Roman colony known as Africa. The entire north strip of the continent from Egypt to Morocco was subjected and militarized to create an uninterrupted frontier, called *limes*, with a twofold objective: protection of fertile agricultural land and defense of the flourishing coastal cities.

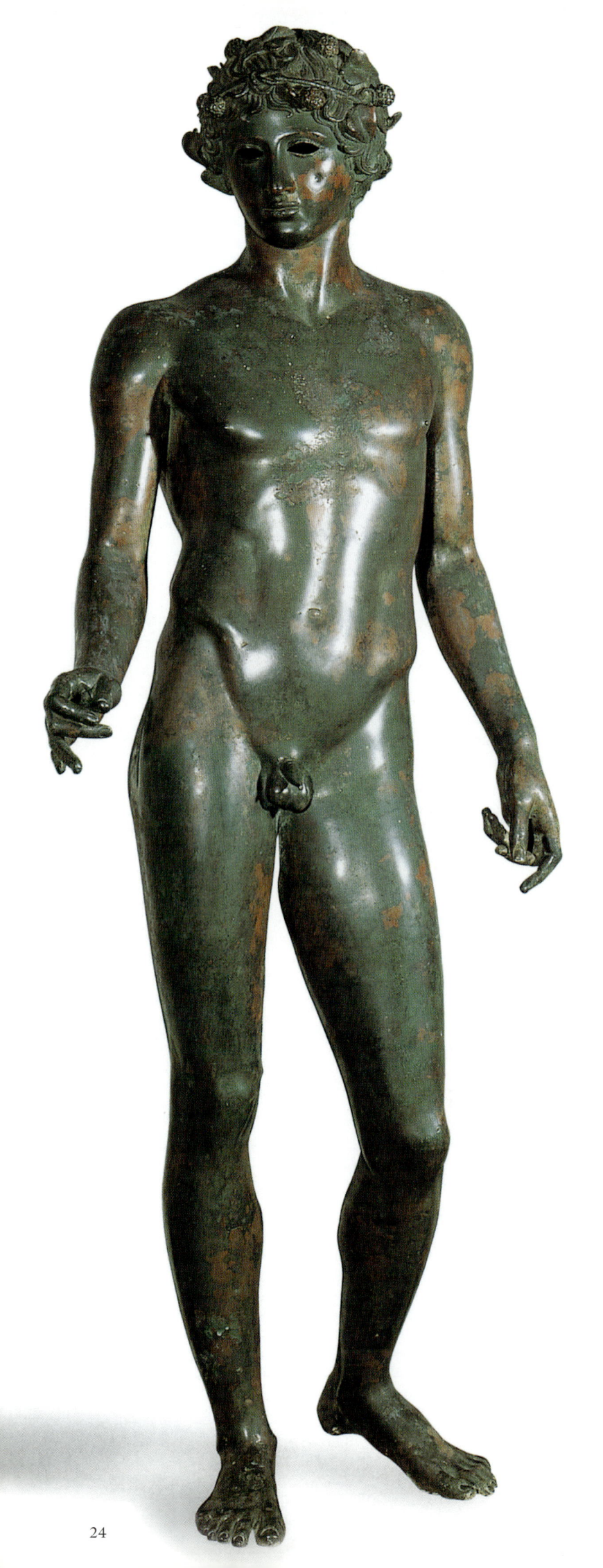

24 left A beautiful bronze ephebe crowned with ivy produced at the start of the imperial era. Although of provincial manufacture, the modeling is very refined and the details remarkable.

24 right and 25 left The two bronzes found at Volubilis show acrobats like those who used to cheer festivals in the Mauritanian capital. Like all the most important objects from prehistoric and pre-Roman sites in Morocco, they are part of the collection at the Archaeological Museum in Rabat.

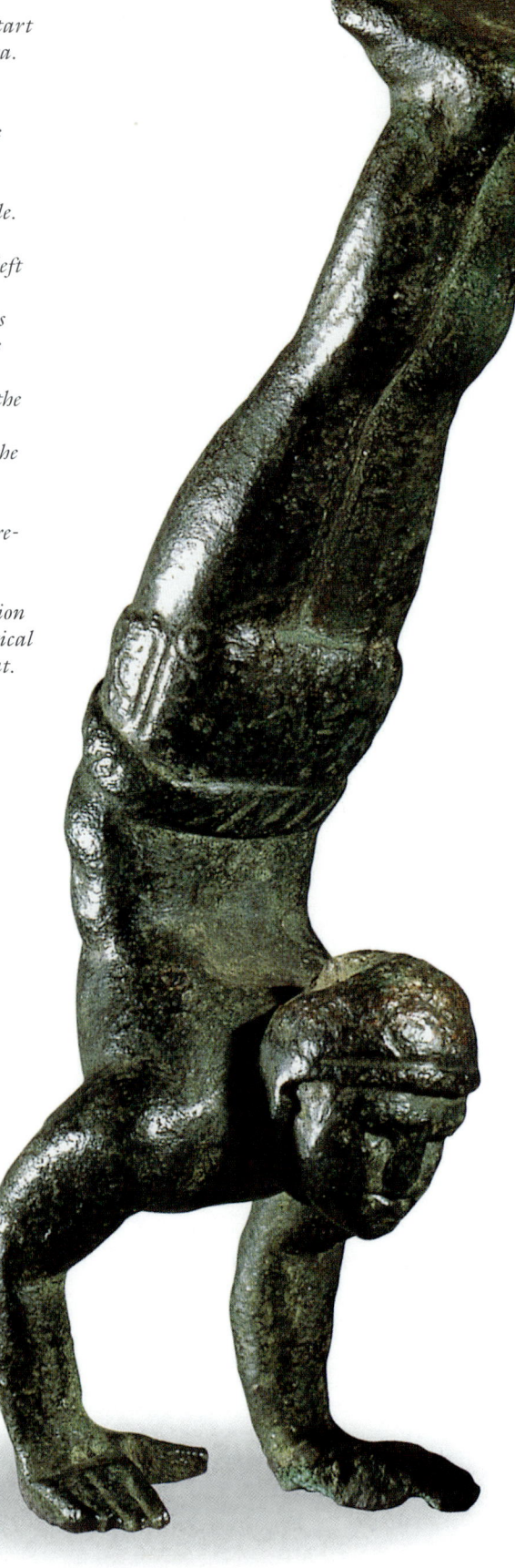

25 right This unusual bronze is known as the "Dog of Volubilis". It measures twenty-five x fourteen inches and was produced in the second century AD. This was the city's period of greatest splendor when thriving trade encouraged the development of the arts.

This process of Romanization brought about the creation of a mixed Mauritanian kingdom that extended from Algeria to Morocco over which the Roman emperor, Augustus, placed the Berber king, Juba II. This was a well-tried formula in the Roman empire that ensured the local state a wide degree of autonomy in return for military control of its frontiers and payment of taxes and tributes, but when Caligula ordered the assassination of Ptolemy, the son of Juba II, in 40 AD, the Berbers rebelled and forced Rome to make a large military intervention. Emperor Claudius succeeded in definitively colonizing the area by dividing it into two provinces: Mauretania Cesarensis to the west and Mauretania Tingitana to the east. The latter extended across most of present day Morocco and had Tingis (modern Tangiers) and Volubilis as capitals. Both provinces supplied Rome with cereals and *porpora*, a purple dye that was produced in particular on the island of Mogador, just off Essaouira. It is said that *porpora* was the cause of Ptolemy's death as he presented himself to Caligula wearing a tunic of this color though it is not known how aware he was that purple was reserved for emperors. The affront, however, was probably an adequate excuse to eliminate the brazen prince.

Civil life in Roman Morocco was decidedly prosperous even if the customs of the empire were essentially limited to the major towns: beautiful Volubilis, Lixus, Cotta, Tamuda, Tingis, Sala and Banasa. Throughout the rest of the provinces, tribal life underwent a single but substantial change: from a fundamentally wandering civilization based on grazing, links were created with land and agricultural activities increased. Another development no less important than ethnic mixing was the spread and dominance of the monotheistic religions of the Mediterranean which the anarchic and individualist spirit of the nomads was prepared to accept but not at the expense of rejecting all other possibile variants.

This was particularly the case with Christianity which became widely accepted but which each tribe interpreted in its own manner. Schisms and sects met with great success, in particular at the start of the fifth century when the Donatist schism seemed to become a national religion.

By then the long Roman influence had waned. By the end of the third century, the southern part of the country had already lost almost all contact with the Empire and the arrival of the Vandals in 429 marked the end of Mauretania Tingitana. It was a period of turbulence that saw Morocco controlled first by a mixed Vandal-Berber-Roman community, then marginally by Byzantium, and, finally and with much more authority, by the Berbers themselves.

The Berbers created a sort of confederate, called *Zenata*, in which borders and rules were very approximate and this turned out to be just a temporary authority as a new power was waiting in the wings: the Arabs soon burst through from the east bringing Islam with them. Their military and religious conquest caused strong resistance and the Berber tribes showed unexpected solidarity. A large coalition was created headed by the famous princess Kahina, "the priestess," and the invaders had to fight hard to overcome the proud and combative nomads. The tribesmen were difficult to flush out in a landscape where they knew the country like the backs of their hands but the Islamic invasion and its successive waves eventually overcame all resistance.

In 682, the Arabs under Oqba Ibn Nafi entered Moroccan territory for the first time and in 702 the Zenata confederation was definitively defeated. Six years later, the country was submitted to the rule of Damascus by Moussa Ibn Nusair. In 711, the invasion continued when Tariq Ibn Ziyad landed in Gibraltar and began the conquest of Spain but even more important than the success of the Arab armies was the arrival of their religion. If, on the one hand, Islam brought a new conception of faith and civil life, it reinforced the nationalist ferment of the Moroccan tribesmen of Berber origin on the other. This state of affairs was strengthened by Kharijism, a religious doctrine that recognized political authority to be directly derived from God. The Khariji doctrine stated that power was to be held by the "best" regardless of their ethnic or social position and the "best" were such if recognized by the mass of believers. This is one way to interpret

26 Planisphere manufactured during the Almohad dynasty when the sciences and geography made great advances. Instruments able to measure the earth were produced for the first time resulting in benefits in political and military administration.

the religion that conquered the Berbers who were convinced they were not only dominant militarily but also religiously.

Another contributing factor was that Islam, being based in the distant cities of Baghdad and Cairo, only provided short-term stability, rarely longer than one or two dynastic generations. Contributing to the rapid turnover of authority and the merry-go-round of empires, wars and conquests were the massive dimensions of the territories the Arabs had conquered and yet could not control militarily. It was an empire in potential only. Because it took months if not years for an army to cross from one country to another, political unity from Asia to the Atlantic could never be a reality. Set against this background, the pride of the Moroccan peoples, their ability as fighters and the agricultural wealth of the country were all factors that had an immediate influence on the political scene which resulted in the rise and fall of a series of powerful dynasties. During the conquest of Spain, Islam's most organized expansion in Europe, the role of the Berber kingdoms was a determining factor not just militarily but also artistically and architecturally.

27 left The Vandals led by Genseric invaded north Africa in 429 AD, putting an end to Roman control of Mauritania Tingitana. Their rule was short and collapsed in 477 with the death of their king.

27 right 1847 lithograph of Tariq Ibn Ziyad by Theodor Hosemann. The Moslem Berber chief landed on Gibraltar in 711 marking the start of the conquest of Spain. In that period, the Islamicization of Morocco was meeting resistance.

In 772, Morocco was ruled by the Abbasid dynasty. This dynasty was faithful to Baghdad and had been pushed into the region after losing a war against the Umayyads but theirs was an ephemeral hegemony as one of Morocco's greatest historical figures, Moulay Idris, was appearing on the horizon. Proclaiming himself a direct heir of Mohammed, he became the leader of the Berber tribes in the north-west and took power in 788. He created the largest single state that had ever existed in Moroccan territory but was killed on the orders of the Abbasid caliph, Harun al-Rashid. The throne passed to his son, Idris II, who further expanded the kingdom and made his capital in Fez, but on his death the country was divided between his heirs and any attempt to unify the country up until the establishment of the Almoravid dynasty was destroyed by internecine

28 left The print portrays Ibn Battuta, a Moroccan geographer and explorer, during a trip to Egypt. His love of exploration and adventure took him to east Africa, India, the Middle East, the Maldives, Sumatra and the ports of China. In old age he wrote an account of his travels.

28 right A gold coin minted during the Almohad dynasty during which the territory of Morocco included Libya, Tunisia, Algeria and part of Spain.

29 The image shows a 13th century miniature of a Moroccan camel-driver. In this period the country experienced a great increase in trade and a flourishing of the arts; the cities became cultural centers that married the spirit of the Arabs with the refinement of the Spanish.

wars, revolts and unexpected occupations by the Umayyads and Tunisians.

The new movement for unification of the country began far away in the western Sahara between Senegal and Niger. Here the Sanhadja tribes, following the religious principles of the theologian Ibn Yasin, gathered their troops together in fortified monasteries - the Ribat - where religious practice went hand in hand with military training. This orthodox Islamic movement was responsible for the Almoravid dynasty that first defeated the black kingdom of Ghana and then reconquered Morocco. A new capital was founded in Marrakesh, the name of which was taken to define the country. The Almoravids were magnificent warriors and, on the wings of success, they crossed the Strait of Gibraltar to Spain, defeated the army of Alfonso V and conquered southern Spain.

These victories gave Youssef bin Tachfin one of the largest kingdoms in the western world. It was an empire founded on religion and tempered by life in the desert and it was apparently unassailable but the sloth of its Andalusian court undermined the dynasty which was eventually toppled by the arrival of a new orthodoxy. The revolt was ignited by the words of Ibn Toumert, an apostle of Sufism and leader of the Masmud Berber tribes of the High Atlas, traditionally rivals of the Sanhadja. Proclaiming himself *El Mahdi* (God's envoy), he preached the rejection of riches and ease and instead that one should follow asceticism and a direct relationship with the transcendent world. Ibn Toumert was responsible for all the ideology of the Almohad dynasty but it was only his heir, Abn-al-Moumen, an able strategist who reigned in Marrakesh in 1147, who succeeded in sweeping the Almoravids out of Morocco. His successor, Yacoub al-Mansour "the Victorious," defeated the Spanish and Portuguese at Alarcos so creating the largest Moroccan empire in history that stretched from southern Europe to Libya. It was a model of good administration and the source of much excellent art and architecture. The Almohads knew how to marry the religious extremism of the Berber tribes with the best of the Arab administrative apparatus in Spain. They set up a centralized administration of great efficiency, the *mahkzen*, and carried out the surveying of all territory in northern Africa. This operation optimized collection of tributes, rationalized agriculture, made possible the financing of a formidable war machine and effectively countered the tendency of the tribes to split up the land. It was a "golden age" that stimulated philosophy - as demonstrated by the physician, jurist and thinker Averroës - but also medicine, botany, geography, music and poetry. It is certainly not incorrect to speak of a "Maghreb school" when considering writers like Abou Hamid al-Gharnati, Ibn Jubair and the incredible writer and traveler Ibn Battuta, the Marco Polo of the Almohads; all the expressive potential resident in Moorish architecture flowered in decorative art giving rise to works of art like the mosques of Marrakesh, Taza and Tin Mal and the Hassan Tower in Rabat.

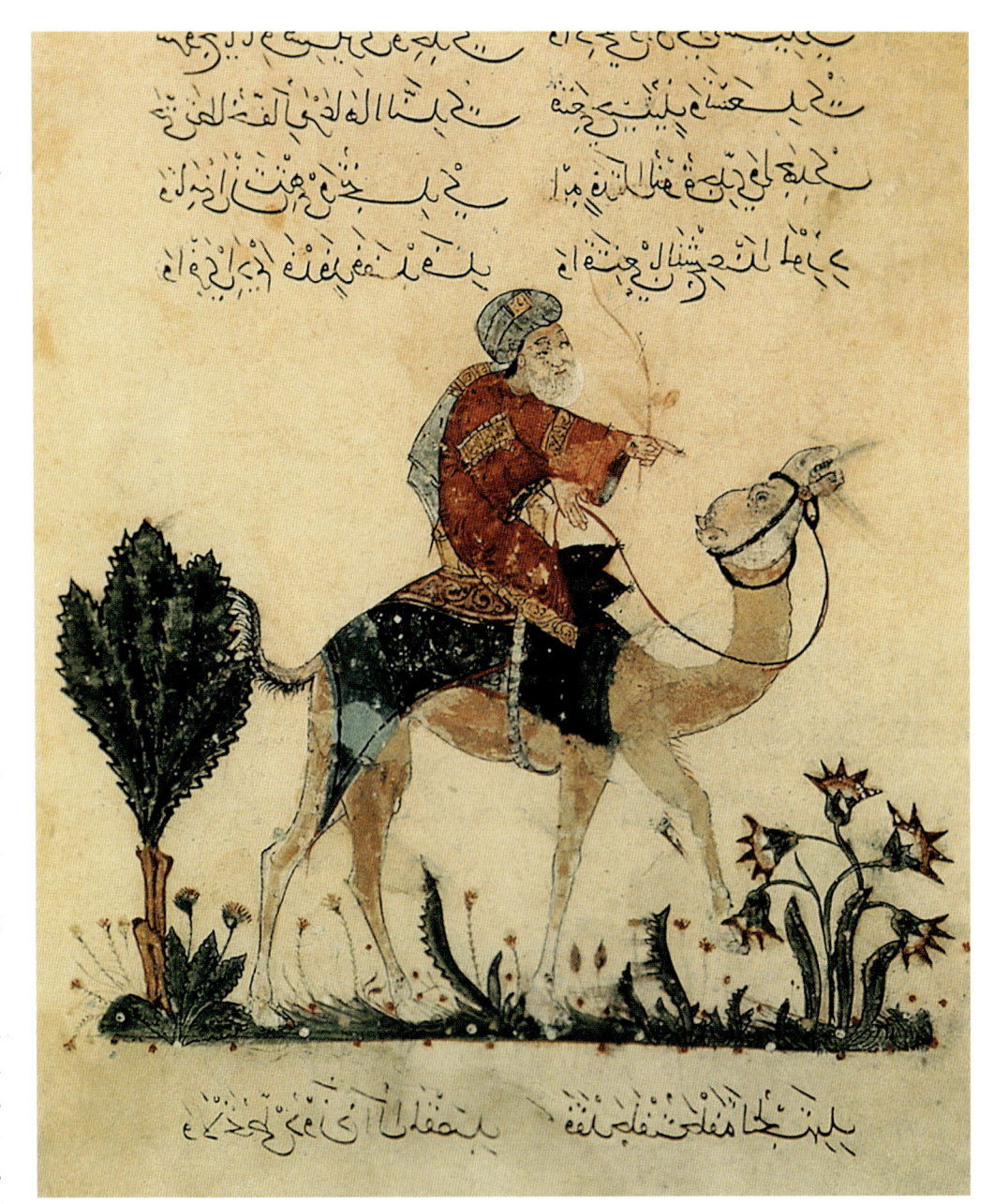

But despite the achievements of the Almohad dynasty, its results were only partial and ephemeral up against the traditional rebellious spirit of the Berber tribes. Their readiness to form factions manifested itself on the first signs of the breaking up of the empire and grew with the passing of power from the Almohads to the Marinids.

The Marinids were a Berber dynasty originally from the land south of Fez that conquered the country between 1216 and 1269. Under this dynasty, arts continued to proliferate and architecture spread into the design of fountains, Turkish baths, caravanserai, bridges, mausoleums and *mederse*, the Koranic schools that trained the ruling lay and religious classes. The aim of these buildings was to celebrate the greatness of the civilization by glorifying its rulers.

In 1492, Granada surrendered and the Iberian peninsula was once more completely Catholic. It was the end of an epoch. Unable to hold the empire together, the Marinids were attacked on two fronts: the revolt of the tribes in the interior which was fired by the flowering of numerous mystical sects averse to more orthodox Islam, and the war that the Spanish and Portuguese had carried across to the Moroccan coast.

One after another the cities of Tangiers, Larache and Agadir fell to the Lusitanians and Melilla was annexed to the Spanish crown. The final defeat of the Marinids presaged the end of Morocco as an autonomous and independent kingdom but this did not actually occur thanks to renewed national and religious pride.

Characteristic are the mausoleums of Chellah designed by the greatest builder of the 14th century, Abou al-Hassan, which signal the apex of Marinid art. But the dynasty was unable to express itself at the same level politically or militarily and it was incapable of cutting back the independent spirit of the tribes; it also suffered a series of setbacks and defeats in Spain.

In 1415, Portugal conquered Ceuta so that, for the first time, a European power possessed land in Moroccan territory.

*30 bottom left
An elegant map of Europe and North Africa drawn in 1381 by Abraham Cresques for Charles V, the king of France. It is now kept in the British Museum. Mapmakers of the period showed Morocco as the point where the two continents ideally met.*

30 bottom right This map of Africa was taken from Ptolemy's Cosmography, a 1486 work; the northern part of the continent is filled with place names but the southern strip is referred to as "Terra Incognita."

30-31 and 31 right This 15th century Portuguese tapestry depicts the disembarkation of Portuguese troops in Tangiers under the leadership of Alfonso V. The Portuguese not only conquered the city but also occupied Larache and Agadir, bringing the Marinid dynasty closer to its end.

Once again the highland tribes were the protagonists.

First the Wattasids led the holy war on behalf of the *marabout*, religious leaders raised to the status of living saints, and then the job was completed by the Arab Sa'di dynasty. This family claimed direct descent from Mohammed and consequently gave its heads the title of *sharif*, successors of the Prophet.

Unexpectedly, the course of history was inverted but the new dynasty had come to power during difficult times; in the Mediterranean, the Catholic powers led by Spain were fighting the powerful Ottoman empire. In particular, the Turks armed fleets of pirates that were active off the coasts of Morocco. Taking advantage of their strategic position in the conflict, the Sa'di were able to consolidate their power decisively. The greatest soldier of the age was the caliph Abn al-Malik, an educated and astute general who inflicted a memorable defeat on the Portuguese at Ksar al Kebir. It was 1578 and Morocco had entered a new era.

Under Ahmed al-Mansour, important new diplomatic relations were undertaken with the most powerful European nations while a policy of conquest over black Africa was begun. In 1590, the ruler sent an army of 4,000 men across the Sahara to defeat the Songhai empire in Gao. The expedition was formed by emigrant Moors from Spain, Turks, renegade Christians and Moroccan horsemen and they were armed with cannon and rifles. This was the first time that fire-arms had made their appearance in Africa and the result was overwhelming. The success of the Sa'di army took the power of the *sharifs* as far as the river Niger and Timbuktu.

32 This 18th century print shows the battle of Ksar al-Kebir in which Caliph Abn al-Malik overwhelmed a Portuguese army of seventeen thousand men. King Sebastian I lost his life in the fighting, an event that marked the end of Portuguese rule in Africa.

33 top This painting on a wooden panel by the German master Tobias Stimmer shows a king from the Sa'di dynasty; it was under these rulers that piracy began to plague Spanish shipping but the Spanish navy was incapable of putting an end to the phenomenon.

33 center This painting from the 19th century Spanish school celebrates the deeds of Charles V's army. The military and political weakness of the Marinid dynasty led to the loss of Granada and, in 1497, to the invasion of Morocco and the conquest of Melilla.

33 bottom An engraving of a sharif of Fez, the sultan of Morocco, during the Sa'di dynasty. The Sa'di rulers boosted the trade in gold and slaves with the use of caravans that crossed the desert.

For almost twenty years the enterprise ensured an uninterrupted flow of gold, spices, ivory and ebony into Marrakesh that made the "Gateway to the Desert" one of the richest cities in North Africa, but, with time, it was seen that the conquest had been a Pyrrhic victory as the commercial system operating in the area had become irremediably compromised and the new developments did not encourage trade at all. Moreover, the forays carried out by the Tuareg made the caravans perilous and the "Atlantic gold route" begun by the Portuguese took away much of the importance of the Saharan traffic.

On the death of Ahmed al-Mansour during a dynastic struggle, the empire folded. An independent republic dedicated to piracy was formed between Rabat and Salè governed by Andalusian emigrants. Power passed from the Sa'di to the Alawites (or Husainites), which was another dynasty that claimed direct descent from the Prophet.

Seventeenth and eighteenth century Morocco was a "hinge" country squeezed between Ottoman imperialism and the European colonial expansion. The power of the rulers depended for the most part on their ability to check the religious unrest and aspirations of independence of the Berber tribes. The empire was only able to maintain its independence by uniting the population behind Islam so that the central authority, although not always divided, was respected for its origin. Its direct association with Mohammed made the population proud, legitimated the dynasty and

34 top Caliph Moulay ar-Rachid was the founder of the Alouite dynasty that still governs Morocco. The monarch, who was of Arab origin and a descendant of the Prophet, unified the country after a brief period of turbulence; he also succeeded in limiting piracy and moved the capital back to Fez.

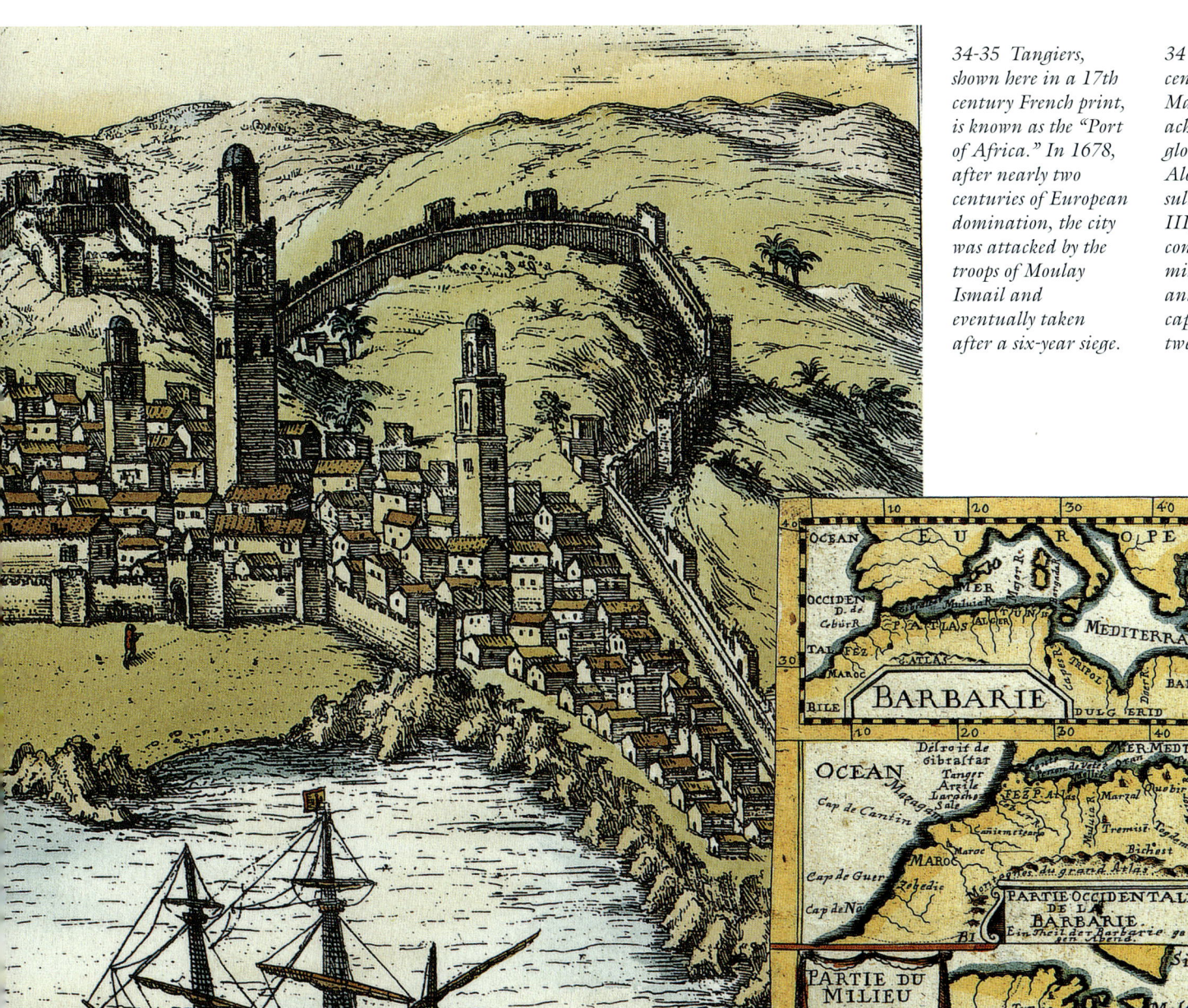

34-35 Tangiers, shown here in a 17th century French print, is known as the "Port of Africa." In 1678, after nearly two centuries of European domination, the city was attacked by the troops of Moulay Ismail and eventually taken after a six-year siege.

34 bottom The 18th century picture shows Marrakesh, which achieved its greatest glory under the Alouite kings. The sultan, Mohammed III, restored the city completely in the mid-18th century and established his capital there for twenty five years.

linked the crown to the main religious authorities. The Moroccan government succeeded in regaining a certain degree of authority under Moulay Ismail and Sidi Mohammed bin Abdallah; good relations were established with European powers, in particular with France under Louis XIV and England under James II. The court refined its customs, trade picked up and Larache and Tangiers were liberated. The war machine was completely reorganized and the use of professional troops became standard whether they were Arabs expelled from Catholic countries or black slaves from west Africa. This meant that Morocco's rulers were always able to count on well-prepared troops able to control the frontier with Senegal or to deal with ambitious tribal chiefs.

During the Alawite dynasty, the capital shifted to Meknes which flourished architecturally, civilly and religiously.

35 center A French map of the 18th century shows North Africa from the Atlantic to Egypt, referred to as "Barbary." It was occupied to the west by the Sa'di kings and to the east by the Ottoman empire.

But the state had no solid base and, on the death of Sidi Mohammed bin Abdallah, the splits began to appear once more. The desire for autonomy of the mountain and desert tribes started to grow, the pirate cities on the coast reaffirmed their independence and power passed to the military chiefs that controlled the Senegalese militias. In addition to all this, a terrible plague swept the country in 1799 killing more than one hundred thousand people. Morocco was a country in crisis and ready to fall to foreign influence.

France, which had recently conquered Algeria, Spain and England all recognized the favorable moment and drew close. It was the French that inflicted the first serious African defeat to the Moroccan forces in 1844 but the situation did not develop into colonial occupation due to the protests of the British. The power of the Alawites, however, was hopelessly undermined. The divisions multiplied and, despite the efforts of sultan Moulay Hassan, Morocco was unable to resist foreign pressure. In fact the sovereign did not control even half of the country and was forced to accept the Treaty of Madrid in 1880 which allowed Morocco to retain formal independence in return for opening its borders to European trade.

36 top Moulay Hassan came to the throne in 1873 and was the last absolute Moroccan king before the country's borders were opened to European trade. During his reign, he attempted to dampen internal revolt and to resist the colonial aims of foreign powers.

36 bottom The painting by Joachin Dominguez shows a negotiation between the Moroccans and the Spanish at the start of the 19th century.

36-37 In 1844 the French armies inflicted a heavy defeat on the Moroccans and Algerians under the rebel Emir Abd al-Kader. Only diplomatic intervention by the British prevented Morocco from losing its independence.

37 bottom This painting by Stefano Ussi shows the arrival of the Italian ambassador in Morocco. All the major European powers established embassies and consulates in Morocco in the mid-19th century.

Le Petit Journal

SUPPLÉMENT ILLUSTRÉ

23ᵐᵉ Année — Numéro 1.137

Dimanche 1ᵉʳ SEPTEMBRE 1912

5 cent. — 5 cent.

ADMINISTRATION
61, RUE LAFAYETTE, 61

Les manuscrits ne sont pas rendus
On s'abonne sans frais
dans tous les bureaux de poste

ABONNEMENTS
SEINE et SEINE-ET-OISE.. 2 fr. 3 fr. 50
DÉPARTEMENTS............ 2 fr. 4 fr. »
ÉTRANGER .... 2 50 5 fr. »

DANS LE SUD MAROCAIN
L'appel aux armes des partisans de Hibba

By the start of the 20th century, Morocco had reached collapse with the population suffering previously unknown levels of poverty. Delinquency became rampant and was only partly stemmed by increasing recourse to the death penalty. Meanwhile, the only trade that prospered was in slaves and the revolts that broke out bloodied the poorly controlled territory in which the population no longer answered to any authority.

Using the excuse that it was necessary to protect its own citizens, France occupied Casablanca in 1907 and four years later entered Fez regardless of the strong protests of Germany which had set its own sights on the country. The intervention, requested by sultan Moulay abd al-Hafid, was necessary to quell a revolt but it opened the door to colonization of Morocco. On March 30, 1912, Morocco was forced to accept a protectorate that safeguarded (though only formally) the autonomy of the state. In reality, the role of the sultan was purely representative while all power lay in the hands of the Resident General Lyautey. At the same time, northern Morocco passed to the Spanish with the protectorate of Tetuan and the international zone was created in Tangiers.

This city, already immortalized by the greatest Orientalist painters, became world famous as a trade center, a free port and a haven of spies and intellectuals through the works of writers such as Paul Bowles, Tennessee Williams, Paul Morand and Jean Genet.

38 In the south of Morocco in 1912, the partisans called on the people to rebel against the French colonial troops.

39 top The Sultan Moulay Youssef was the first Moroccan ruler to attempt sharing power with the French.

39 center left The Algeciras Conference of 1906 established areas of influence for the European powers in Morocco.

39 center right In 1912, Moulay Ab al-Hafid permitted his country to become a French protectorate, then abdicated in favor of his brother Moulay Youssef.

39 bottom Louis H.G. Lyautey, French Resident-General of Morocco from 1912 to 1925, had the task of restoring order within the country. He appointed French staff to work with the local administration, accelerated the processes of modernization and chose Rabat as the capital.

41 top French troops on camelback in winter 1937 move in the direction of Spanish Morocco. The presence of armed German forces in the colony during the years before World War II created moments of serious tension along the borders.

41 bottom Abd al-Krim, the charismatic tribal chief of the Rif, defeated the Spanish in 1921 and proclaimed independence. After invading the French possessions and threatening Fez, he was defeated and imprisoned but managed to escape to Egypt. He died in exile in 1963 and is still considered a great national hero.

40 top Spanish cavalry troops prepare to salute during exercises. In 1936, Franco's Falangists, who had rebelled against the Spanish government, gathered the support of 130,000 soldiers in Morocco.

40-41 French troops in combat during the occupation of Morocco. Between 1912-1932 the Atlas and the Sahara regions were a ferment of uprisings and rebellions; it is thought that in these two decades 400,000 Moroccans and 27,000 French soldiers lost their lives.

With the rapid modernization of the coast, problems there ceased but control of the interior created enormous difficulties for the European powers. Revolts in the Rif mountains and Middle Atlas severely tested the colonial armies. In twenty years of clashes, the French lost 27,000 men and the Moroccans 400,000. In 1921, the tribes of the western Rif led by Abd al-Krim soundly defeated a Spanish army of 15,000 soldiers and proclaimed themselves independent. They were only forced to surrender by a combined Spanish and French force of 250,000 men equipped with artillery, planes and poison gas. Abd al-Krim, who died in exile in 1963, is still considered a hero in the Rif.

42 top The portrait is of Mohammed V, the king who, from 1947, showed he was sympathetic to nationalist movements and refused to obey French directives. By 1956, he had led the country back to full independence.

42 bottom The funeral of Mohammed V took place in Rabat on February 28, 1961 in front of one million people. The new king, Hassan II (wearing sunglasses in the foreground) led the procession. Despite the huge crowd, the ceremony is still remembered for its simplicity.

The watershed for the nationalist movement coincided with World War II; the Moroccan population barely tolerated the Vichy regime and, in 1942, welcomed the Anglo-American troops warmly.

Five years later, sultan Mohammed II declared himself favorable to the nationalist movement and began an unwavering struggle with the French authorities that ended with his exile. By this stage the country was no longer governable and the revolts became ever bloodier until, in 1955, the sultan was allowed to return to Morocco.

In 1956, the country regained its full freedom; on March 2 the declaration of independence from the French zone was signed and on

able politician, Hassan II lived in an aura of myth: inflexible with his opponents, he was able to protect Morocco from the Islamic extremism that has affected other countries in the region. The controversy over the Rio de Oro, however, has always been a ticklish and unresolved matter. For over twenty years, Morocco has been bogged down in the complex political and military situation of the Western Sahara.

April 7 the Spanish protectorate was annexed. Immediately the new country had to face two difficulties: attacks on ex-collaborationists of the French government and the loss of foreign capital in search of safer investments.

In 1961, Hassan II assumed the throne. He was responsible for the modernization of the country and the creation of Morocco's first constitution in 1962. A powerful and

43 center Moroccans are held back by French troops as they protest against the visit to Meknès of the Resident-General, Gilbert Grandval. The visit to the city of the colonial power's representative sparked a revolt resulting in sixteen dead and forty-nine injured.

43 top The first official speech by King Hassan II was given in Rabat on April 3, 1961. The king launched a plan for the modernization of the monarchy so that it would be in a position to deal with the task of running the country.

43 bottom The first elections after the restoration of independence were held in 1956. The government was installed in Rabat by royal appointment but had difficulty in functioning due to the fragmentation of the political forces.

In 1975 the government organized the famous "Green March" claiming possession of the territory and lined the border with an immense crowd of three hundred fifty thousand men but when Spain left the colony, Morocco was obliged to tackle the fiery resistance of the inflexible Sahrawi people who claimed their independence under the banner of the Polisario Front. Since then, the efforts of the UN to impose a referendum have come to nothing.

On the financial front, growth has been very slow and high unemployment forced a sizeable percentage of the local work force to emigrate.

Today, however, the situation has notably improved. Morocco is on the whole a modern country, politically aligned with western governments and its economy is in slow but constant growth. In 1997, the first elections with universal suffrage were held. The result was a delicate balance with the coalition of the four opposition parties, Koutla Addimocratia, winning 102 seats against the one hundred of the right wing supporters of the government, the Wifaq group. A further ninety-seven seats were won by center parties. Following these results, King Hassan II appointed the leader of the Socialist Union of the Forces of the People, Abderrahman Youssoufi, as prime minister in February 1998. These developments testify that Morocco is offering its people an open and articulated political system, certainly among the most modern and liberal in North Africa.

This is confirmed by the flowering of important literary talents, some of whom are known beyond the country's borders: Mohammed Choukri, Dris Chraibi, Mohammed Kheir-Eddine, Ahmed Sefrioui and, above all, Tahar bin Jelloun.

In 1999, the death of Hassan II, an influential sovereign who was always deeply involved in the kingdom's home and foreign policy, marked the end of the old era, as well as the promising consolidation of a new era. In 2002 new parliamentary elections were held and in 2003 the municipal elections, opening the path for today's 33,000,000 Moroccans to place their trust in the young Mohammed VI, in the awareness that they can rely on him for their hopes of stability and modernization for Africa's oldest realm.

44 top Moroccan troop station on the border with Mauritania during clashes in 1987 against the Polisario Front. Despite diplomatic efforts, the situation is still a dangerous one.

44 bottom The 'Green March' was held in 1975 when Spain decided to withdraw from its possessions in the Western Sahara. Three hundred fifty thousand volunteers marched into the ex-colony demanding it be annexed to Morocco.

44-45 King Hassan II of Morocco died on Sunday, July 25, 1999. His thirty-eight-year reign had made him one of the leaders of state that had greatly characterized the history of North Africa. He reigned with great firmness and was inflexible with internal opposition; he succeeded in resisting religious fundamentalism and brought the country closer to the West.

45 top Mohammed VI leaves the mosque of Ahl-Fes and the royal palace in Rabat on the new king's first official outing. A new era was beginning for Morocco, typified by the alternation of political forces in the government.

48 bottom left There are no towns of any size on the Atlantic coast beyond Agadir with the exception of the small port of Tarfaya. Here it seems that the desert reaches all the way to the sea. These were the landscapes that inspired Saint-Exupéry in his story The Little Prince.

Of its 2175 mile length, the shores of the Mediterranean and the stretch down to Casablanca are the most densely populated but as one goes further down the immense Atlantic front, man's presence is thinned leaving simple natural settings of great beauty. Moving from east to west, the coastline as far as the Strait of Gibraltar is mostly rocky with steep, rugged cliffs. Once past Tangiers, huge terraces along the coast contain hundreds of sinks that collect sea water when the tide comes in. When the sea withdraws, the flat bottomed "wells" ringed by crests are left holding fish that are easy prey for sea birds.

The further south one travels down the Atlantic coast, the larger the beaches become. The most famous, at Agadir, have the curious phenomenon of summer fog caused by thermal excursion.

48 top The unspoiled beaches of Tamrhakht and Tarhazout to the north of Agadir are some of the loveliest in south Morocco. The rocky outcrop of Cap Ghir visible in the distance marks the end of the bay.

48-49 The coast turns bare and harsh again to the south of Agadir after the greenery of Wadi Massa oasis. Tall cliffs fall directly into the Atlantic Ocean in this zone.

49 top right and bottom North of Agadir, the seabed ideal for diving and spontaneous vegetation characterize the coastline. The rugged rocks of the coast open into small inlets.

At dawn, the coast is covered by a layer of vapor that varies in density from day to day and which only evaporates in the early afternoon. The land along the Atlantic coast has been marked by the many advances and retreats of the ocean over the centuries; the result is the numerous dry, bare cliffs that stand sometimes many hundreds of feet from the shore.

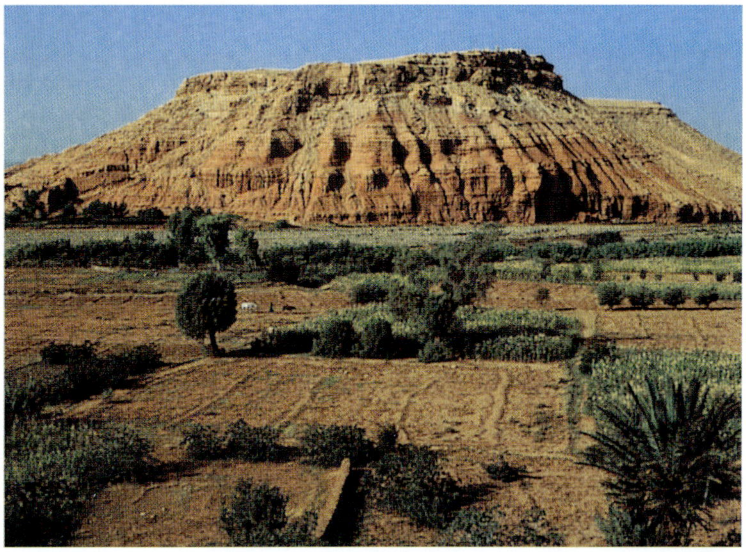
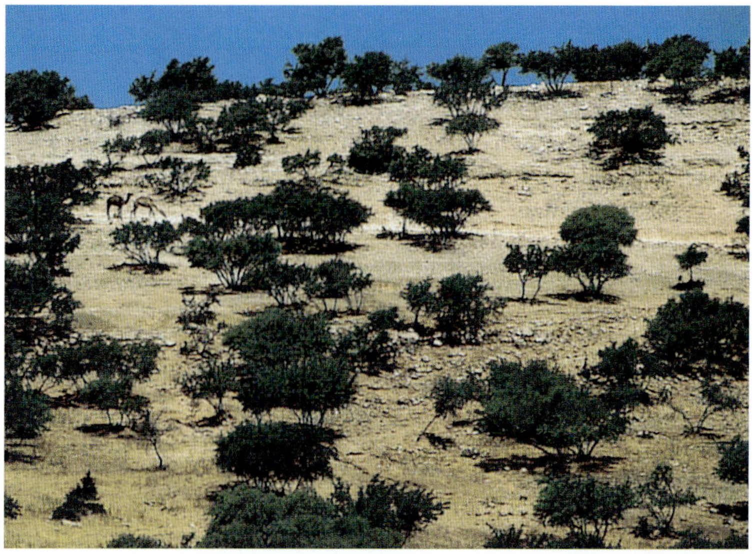
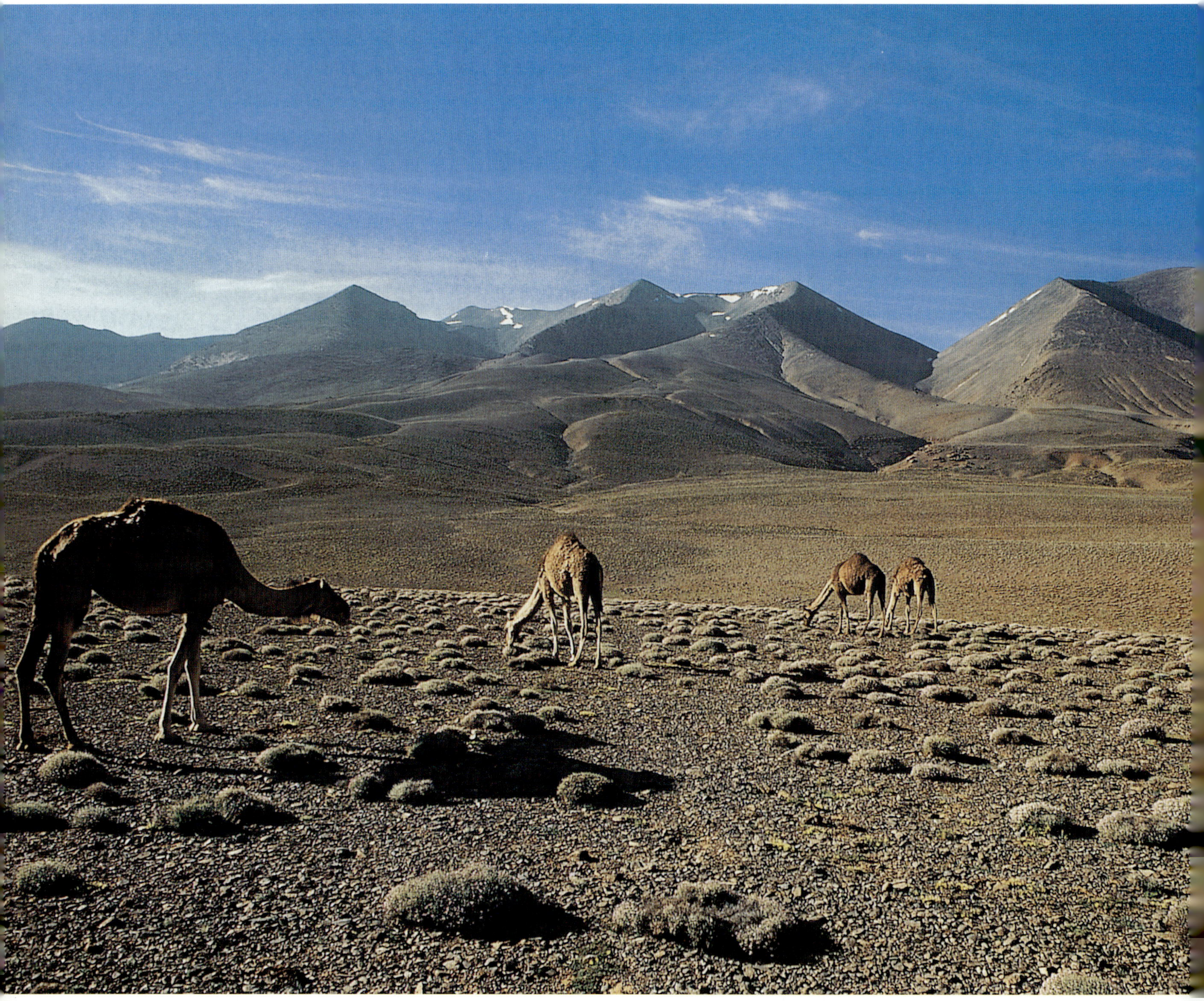

50 top left Route P31 from Marrakesh to Ouarzazate is one of the most scenic in inland Morocco. It winds between the valleys and meadows of the High Atlas, passing fortified towns of austere beauty.

50 top right A typical landscape in the area between Agadir, Tiznit and Ouarzazate. The only trees able to find nourishment in the arid soil are "Morocco ironwood" which grow in great numbers on the steppes.

50-51 Dadès valley rises towards the High Atlas where the Ighil Mgoun massif reaches a height of 13,360 feet. The only people to make use of the land are the nomads with their camel herds.

51 top right The valley of the Ouarzazate lies at the foot of the High Atlas; habitually swept by a strong wind, it offers a landscape of rough beauty. The rock formations are often marked by striations, which indicates the power of the elements.

Just as the bareness inland seems to be definitely almost lunar, south of Agadir, the green strip of Wadi Massa appears. This is a large river oasis that has long been protected as a national park. It is one of Morocco's richest habitats for flora and fauna. The harsh and barren Atlantic hinterland that stretches up to the spurs of the High Atlas and Anti Atlas mountains offers two areas where the landscape is gentler and vegetation takes the upper hand: the extensive woods of argania trees and the forest of Mamora.

The woods grow at an altitude half way up the mountains in areas between Essaouira, Agadir, Tiznit and Ouarzazate, up the valley of the river Sous and among the mountains of the south. The tree is the argania spinosa and is well adapted to the dry, misty terrain. Although it is found in abundance in its wild state, the argania is also cultivated for the perfumed oil extracted from its seeds. In this zone, as elsewhere in foothills, the vegetation varies with altitude so that in the space of just a few miles, the argania trees give way, in order, to pistachio, thuja, cork-oak and holm oak, then juniper and the Atlas cedar. This subtle change alters the colors of the scenery, brings new smells and reveals the progressive severeness of the terrain as the land rises towards the heights of the interior.

Mamora forest, with its 212 square miles of eucalyptuses, acacias and cork oaks, is an enormous green lung located around Rabat, Kenitra and Meknes. The forest is a natural habitat for chameleons and many species of non-migratory birds but it is slowly and inexorably shrinking. Disappearance of forests was, very long ago, perhaps the cause of the creation of the steppes that cover of thousands of square miles in the shelter of the mountains and overlooking the desert, where the landscape is arid and stretches to the horizon. Scoured by the wind and its fertility diminished by lack of rain, which may be non-existent from one year to the next, the steppes are colored every shade of brown and ochre and appear to burst into flame at sunset. The expanses stretch into infinity offering a spectral panorama in which only the distant rise of the mountains gives any sense of direction. Yet, despite their apparent harshness, the steppes are home to many forms of life, for example, short trees and plants that bring beauty to the scene with a short-lived but violent blossoming in spring, and small animals that hide by day and come out at night to hunt for food and search for water. This is the home of geckos and the mastigure, a large prehistoric-looking lizard, but the real king of the steppe is the black-backed jackal, a silent and furtive predator that operates by moonlight.

51 bottom right Note the effects of the harvesting of cork on this cork oak; the "soft cork" suitable for industrial processing is removed manually every nine years.

51

52 top left The gentle vegetation and orderliness of the farming on the green hills that dominate the countryside near Ceuta are reminiscent of Europe.

52 bottom left Often cedar woods are so thick they seem to be a forest. It is calculated that this tree covers an area of 130,000 hectares.

It is indispensable to the ecological balance and offers raw materials to cabinet-makers and makers of stringed instruments.

52-53 Huge fields of maize in the highlands of Tisouka are a successful example of Morocco's growth in farming. Since independence, Morocco has become one of North Africa's largest farm producers.

53 top left The simple houses of a Berber village on the slopes of the Rif to the south of Ketama. The zone has adequate water resources and is one of the most densely populated rural areas in Morocco.

53 top right Farming has flourished on the slopes of the Rif. Annual production of corn – often overseen by co-operatives – has reached 3.6 million tons. Note the typical haystacks in the photograph.

Whether arriving from the desert or more fertile areas, the approach to the mountains is characterized by cedar woods that exist between 3940 and 9186 feet above sea level. The vegetation at this altitude is thick, a green wall of conifers that can reach a height of 162 feet and on occasion grow to 195 feet. The slopes of the Rif, Middle and High Atlas are home to plenty of cedar creating wonderful scenery that seems both Alpine and African.

When considering Morocco as a "hinge" country, i.e. as a bridge between different continents, it is in these forests that the most curious synthesis of the two worlds is to be found. The climate, cool and temperate for most of the year, the light and the color of the leaves may appear European but the wildlife that lives there soon corrects this mistaken impression and pulls us back to Africa with a jerk. The thick vegetation is ideal for the many colonies of Barbary apes which are desirable prey for the last few leopards and the more numerous genets.

Beyond the cedar woods lie the four huge chains of mountains, each with its own characteristics. The Rif stretches across the north of the country from Tetuan to Cap des Trois Fourches near Melilla. It is the least high but serves as a geological and climatic division between Europe and Africa. Its heart lies in the mountains between Chechuan and Al Hoceima all of which are over 6562 feet high.

The wetter slopes that face the Atlantic are covered with rich vegetation while the more arid and wild slopes facing the Mediterranean are decidedly less hospitable. Here the rock walls slope steeply down almost to the sea where narrow inlets, difficult to reach, offer glorious views.

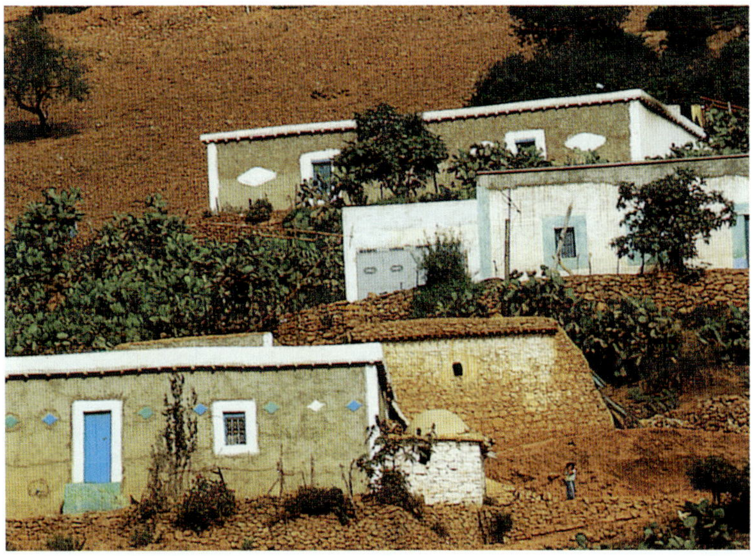

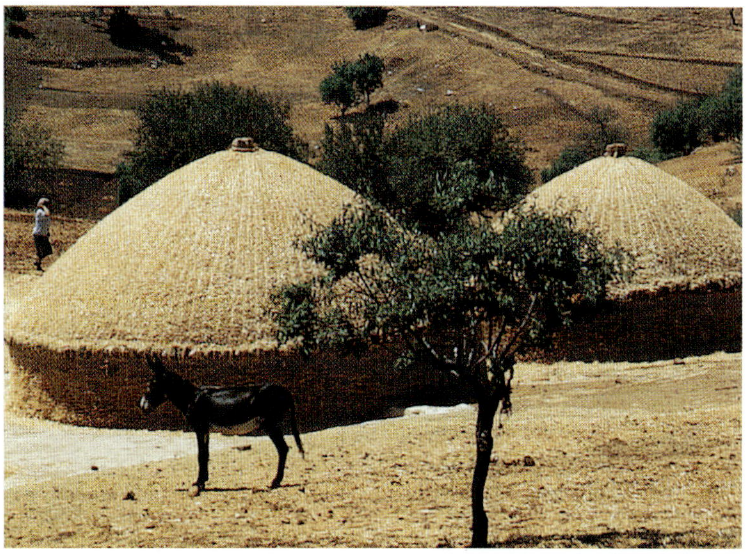

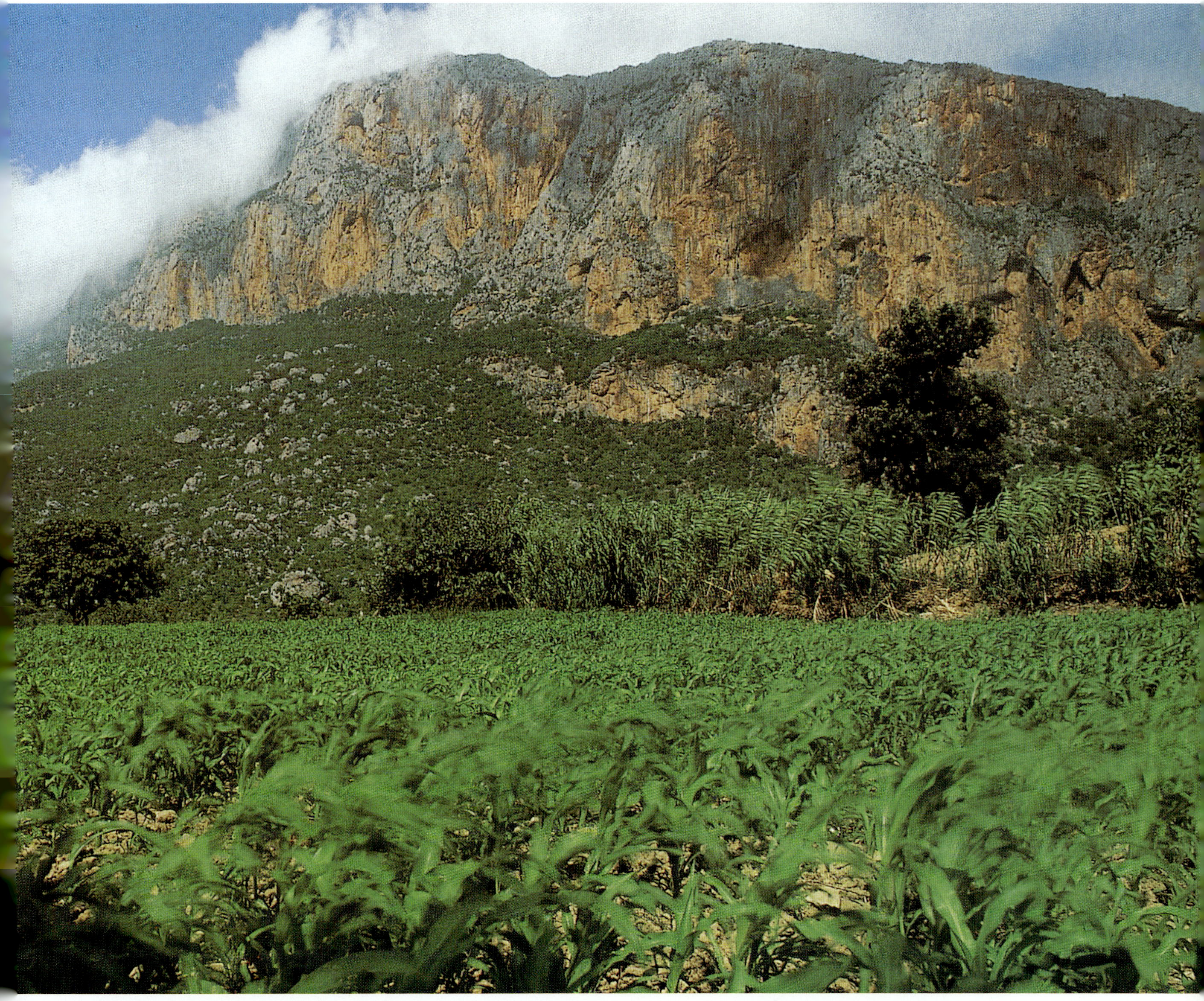

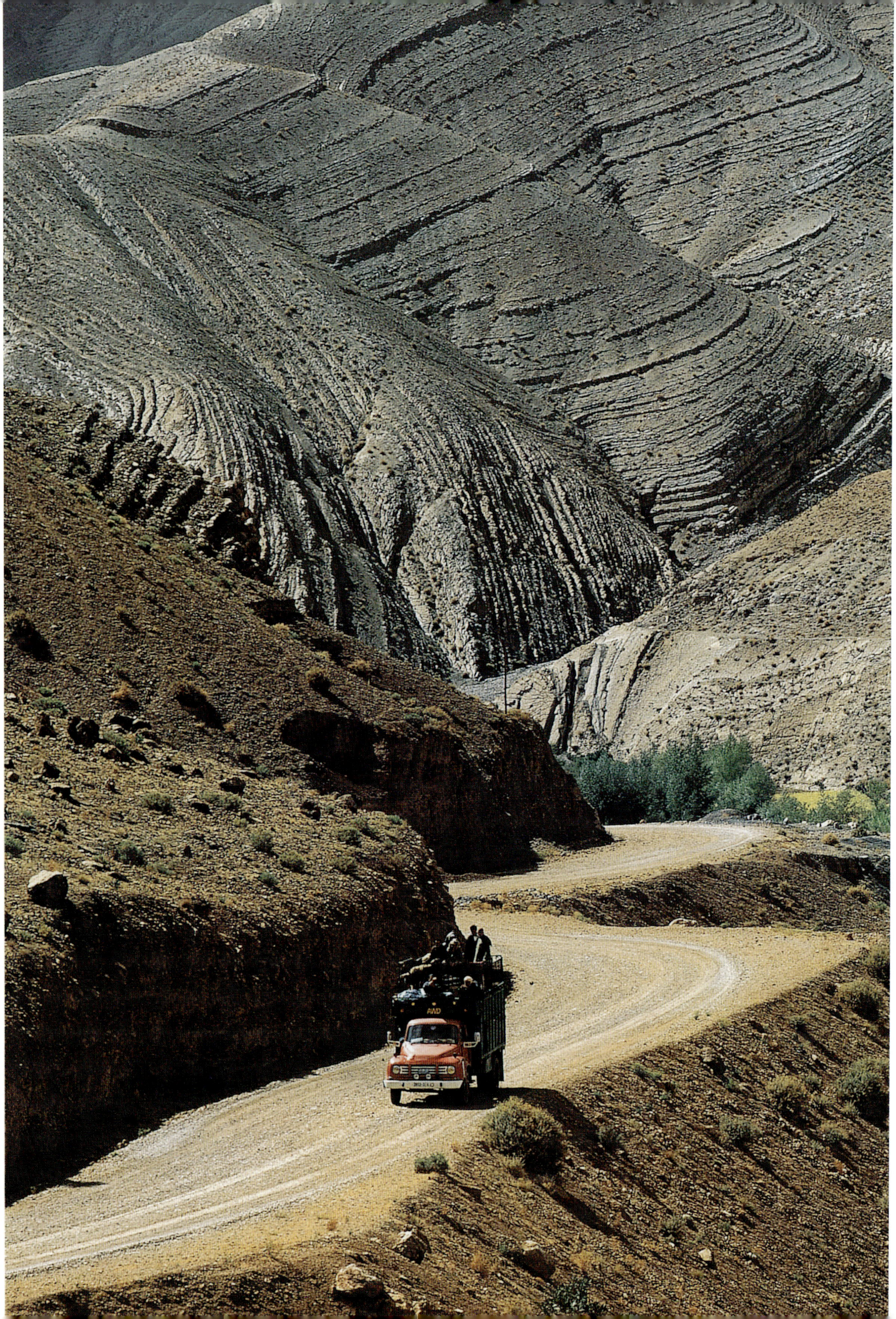

54 The road that twists through the gorges of the Dadès valley offers views of surreal beauty. Steep rock walls and crests stretch out of sight at every turn.

55 top left Ouzoud waterfall drops over three hundred feet in two leaps. Its beauty is heightened by the presence of a permanent rainbow that is clearly seen by those bathing in the pool below.

55 bottom left The area around Tizi N'Tichka pass is a strategic location controlled by local tribes. A famous moussem (pilgrimage) takes place each year in the village of Moulay Brahim to celebrate the birth of the Prophet.

55 top right The Middle Atlas is the location of the country's largest water reserves: rivers and lakes shape and soften the terrain. At higher altitudes, where the peaks approach ten thousand feet in height, the landscape is bare and inhospitable.

55 bottom right The broad expanses of the Middle Atlas are marked by limestone mountain ranges shaped by fractures and karst features.

To the west, the Middle Atlas crowns the central section of the Moroccan Meseta. The highest altitudes are reached in the middle of the chain where rainfall and flora are scarce. The highest peaks are Djebel Bou Naceur at 10,960 feet and Mousa ou Salah in the Bou Iblane massif at 10,466 feet.

The mountains of the western Middle Atlas are much lower, rarely reaching 6562 feet, but they enjoy a better climate with abundant rain. Some of the country's loveliest expanses of cedar and hazelnut trees cover these flanks and several important rivers have their sources here: the Sebou, the Bou Regreg, the Oum ar Rbia and the Moulaya. Receiving so much water, this zone of the Middle Atlas has created many small lakes and scores of streams that contain enough fish to attract tourists.

Overall, the Middle Atlas offers some of Morocco's most beautiful natural settings, especially around Azrou, Ifrane (a winter sports resort), Kenifra and Imilchil near the Plateau des Lacs, a tableland enclosed by mountains that exceed 9842 feet.

56 top left Tizi N'Tichka pass lies at a height of 7415 feet. It is a natural passage that joins Marrakesh to Ouarzazate over the High Atlas. The twisting road that cuts through it (now tarmacked) is of great commercial and strategic importance, and has always been so, despite the obstacles posed by the terrain.

56 bottom left A farmer follows a mule track in Toubkal National Park, which is an ideal starting point for climbing parties in the High Atlas. The French Mountaineering Club runs an inn and three mountain huts that are used as bases for the more difficult ascents.

56-57 Toubkal massif is the highest peak in northern Africa but its many deep and narrow valleys are dangerous in winter and cause many problems to excursionists.

57 top left The paths that lead to Tizi N'Tichka pass are used regularly by shepherds to move their flocks up and down the mountains. From the villages, some as high as 3562 feet, the flocks are led to the pastures of the High Atlas.

57 top right The valleys of the High Atlas are deep and wide, rather like plateaux, and more suitable for man and human occupation. The climate is less harsh making habitation and farming possible.

But the High Atlas is the setting for the highest peaks in North Africa and spectacular natural scenery like no other in this part of the continent. The extraordinary landscape offers deep valleys, permanently snow-capped summits, vertiginous canyons, jagged crests, and sharp peaks eroded by the winds.

The chain stretches 435 miles from Cap Rhir to Djebel Meskakaour on the boundary with the eastern Meseta and includes more than forty mountains over 9843 feet in height. The most impressive is the squat Djebel Toubkal, the highest point in North Africa at 13,701 feet, gouged by deep, inaccessible valleys. Almost as impressive is Ighil Mgoun at 13,356 feet which looks like a gigantic dome scarred with steep, narrow grooves.

Other peaks worthy of mention are Djebel Ouanoukrim (13,415 feet), Djebel Ayachi (12,260 feet), the highest mountain in the central High Atlas, and Djebel Siroua (10,840 feet) which almost borders the Anti Atlas. Throughout winter, temperatures are very low and snowfalls are heavy although no single perennial glacier exists in all the chain.

57

58 top left The highlands of the High Atlas sometimes appear like lunar landscapes, with long series of rounded spurs that stretch out of sight. Note the ruins of a fort that are almost camouflaged against the scenery.

58 center left Lovely Lake Oukaimeden lies in a valley in the buttresses of the High Atlas. The area has a well-known winter sports village and more than one hundred thousand prehistoric rock carvings.

*58 bottom left The small rural houses typical of the High Atlas usually line a river (*wadi *in Arabic) and are red like the local earth.*

58-59 The landscape of the High Atlas is not all steppes and rocky peaks. There are also wide green valleys where more fertile soil provides a base for the intensive cultivation of wheat and vegetables.

Rainfall is frequent on the northern and western uplands so that vegetation is luxuriant but the southern slopes are arid and almost completely barren. The most striking scenery is not easily reached and the roads are difficult to pass, especially during the cold season. Like most of Morocco's mountainous terrain, the High Atlas is thinly populated but this does not lessen its attraction, on the contrary. Descending the valley just a little, the hand of man is clearly apparent in the first villages where he has patiently built up carefully irrigated agricultural terracing. The small patches of vegetation in the midst of the bare solemnity of the mountains are the first sign that a new landscape is close by.

59 top left Natural rock sculptures in the area around Tizi N'Tichka. The pass (also known as the 'Pastures Pass') can be reached via Morocco's highest road.

59 top right Oued Melloul valley is home to rural centers whose simple economy is made possible by the abundance of water.

59

*60 top left
The fortified city of Taroudant is strategically located between the Anti and High Atlas and dominates access to the Sous valley. Rows of eucalyptus, olives and palms lie around its ochre bastions.*

*60 bottom left
The Plateau de la Tessaout lies below the snowy peak of Ighil Mgoun, the highest peak in the High Atlas at over 13,125 feet. The plateau is green and flat, ideal for grazing.*

60-61 The river Draa winds through a fertile valley where oleanders, acacia and date palms are grown. The green strip is further exploited by its inhabitants with the cultivation of vegetables, cereals, medicinal herbs and henna.

61 top left The Anti Atlas often offers views of barren beauty. This photograph taken near the fortified village of Ait Benhaddou shows the last patches of vegetation as the altitude rises.

61 top right Almond trees in bloom and sharp pink granite rocks form an enchanting combination in the mountains surrounding Tafraout and Ousmenat. In this area of the Anti Atlas, the beginning of summer is celebrated with colorful traditional events.

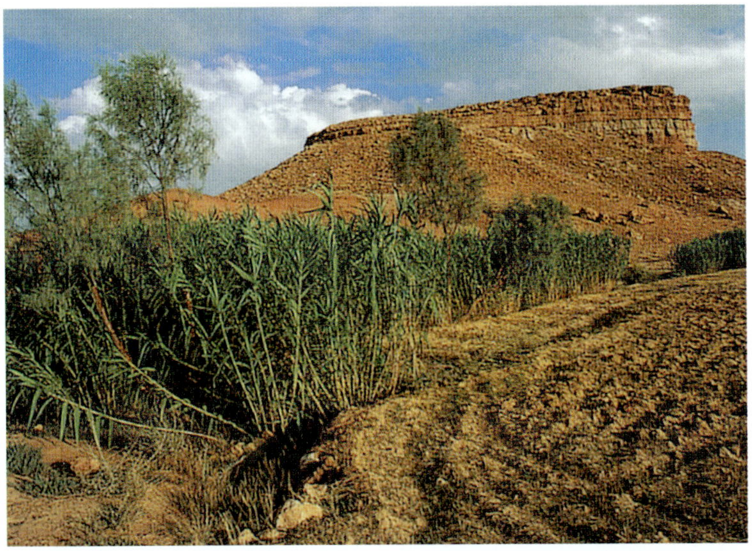
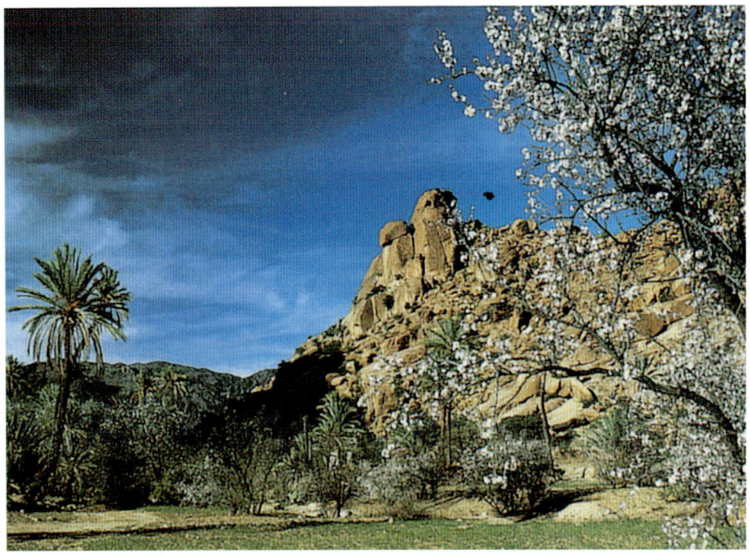
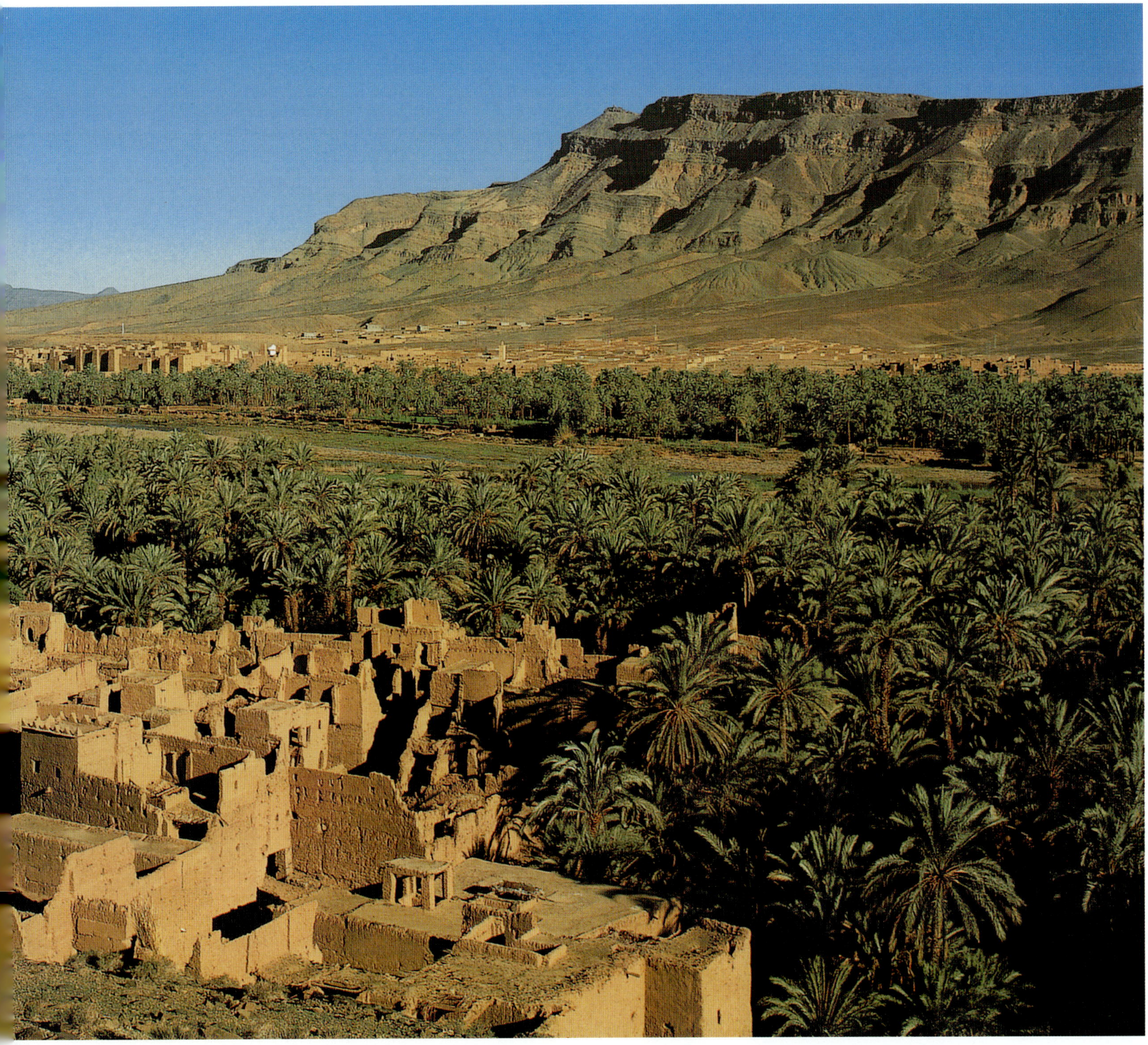

62 and 62-63 Numerous fortified centers were built by local peoples in the Draa valley in defence against raids from desert nomads. There are about fifty of these constructions, called kasbah *or* ksour, *between Ouarzazate and Zagora.*

63 top The mountain landscape of the Anti Atlas near Tafraout is dotted with small farming villages and palm groves. Granite is the local stone, sometimes streaked with delicate shades of pink.

The Anti Atlas is the fourth mountain chain in the country; it is also the oldest and, for many reasons, the least known. Rather than a series of mountain peaks, this is a highland region marked by many wide valleys formed over the centuries by the water of rivers that are now completely dry. Its highest points reach 4921 feet in the west and touch 6652 feet in the east. The

63 center right The red houses in the village of Ousmenat in the Ameln valley cling to the slope of a granite mass. The ancient hamlet seems crushed by the mountain but, in its turn, it looks down on a palm grove with lovely gardens.

64

64 top left Legend has it that the lions of Atlantis still live in the ravines of the Dadès valley but more reliable historical records agree that the last one was killed at the start of the 20th century.

64 top right Maize is one of the highly developed crops in the Dadès valley but it is for the high quality roses grown here that the area is famous internationally.

64-65 Ait Arbi kasbah seems to grow out of the volcanic rock. Not only the color is similar, but also the shape of the fortifications gives the impression that it owes more to nature than to the hand of man.

65 top The Dadès valley offers marvelous views; its greenery is due to the artificial lake formed by the Al-Mansour Eddahbi dam built during the 1970s and to a massive replanting program.

65 bottom The ravines in the Todra valley are the most spectacular in Morocco. The narrow Todra flows into Wadi Rheriss.

tallest elevations are Adrar n'Aklim (8304 feet) and Djebel Lekst (7740 feet).

The northern slopes fall steeply away towards the Sous plain but, to the south, the approach to the desert is much more gentle. The Anti Atlas is pretty dry with only scrub growing on most of it but to the north, in the beds of the dried up rivers, arganias, acacias and euphorbia grow.

The northern peaks are absolutely arid and the area continually suffers from problems linked to lack of water but the scene in the plain enclosed by the mountains of the High and Anti Atlas is very different. Here the waters of the river Sous, which has its sources in the massif of Djebel Siroua, descend to the valley engorged by the many other streams from nearby mountains. The valley's image of carefully cultivated fertility is evident from the groves of cedar, banana, olive and almond that thrive on its banks. This is some of the thickest and healthiest vegetation in the country despite its intense exploitation.

From a scenic point of view, the prettiest area in the Anti Atlas are the Tafraout–Tiznit and Tafraout–Ait Baha stretches of the Ammeln valley with its granite rock.

66 The immense dunes of Erg Chebbi close to Merzouga oasis are the highest to be seen in Morocco. They are constantly being reshaped by the wind and stretch as far as the horizon.

67/70 The solemn gait of camels through the dunes brings to mind the age of the great caravans when the trading journeys across the desert could take months.

71 Erfoud oasis is an ideal base for trips into the Moroccan desert. Watered by Wadi Ziz and Wadi Rheriss, it offers the coolness and refreshment of a palm grove. Each year in October, the Festival of the Date Palms is held here.

FROM THE IMPERIAL CITIES TO THE GATEWAY TO THE DESERT

CASABLANCA, SKYSCRAPERS AND TRADITION

74 top Place Zallara is the heart of the modern city. Casablanca is the most ambitious and economically advanced face of Morocco. It is the shopping and financial center of North Africa.

74 center Place Mohammed V forms the hub around which the most important streets of Casablanca radiate.

74 bottom With a population of over 3.5 million inhabitants, Casablanca is the largest city in the country. It is modern, bustling and the location of North Africa's largest port and Morocco's largest airport. It is the city where important international companies have their headquarters.

Whether overlooking the coast, built on fertile land inland or guarding crossings, passes and caravan routes, the cities of Morocco provide fascinating evidence of the history of this empire which for many years was the most powerful and refined in northern Africa. Today it is a kingdom that balances economic development against tradition, and religion against the lay activities of commerce and cultural exchange with Europe across the water. It is natural to start a description of the cities from the coast where the Berbers first confronted the peoples that arrived by sea – the Phoenicians, Romans, Spanish, Portuguese and French – and where history has become tangible in the form of forts, palaces, intricate city centers, ports and mosques. The glories and tragedies of the Morocco of the past are mirrored in the Morocco of today where cars, shops and televisions mark the rhythm of modern life.

Casablanca is the perfect example. With over 3.5 million inhabitants, it is not only the country's most modern city but also the largest. Progress has decidedly taken the upper hand here, as seen in the central Place Mohammed V from which large streets fan out lined with cinemas, western style shops, offices and banks in an unstoppable march towards modernity. Yet from the same square, one reaches the medina (the old city), the heart of traditional Casablanca. But it is a heart under siege from the modern build-

74-75 The Law Courts face onto Place Mohammed V. The square that forms the elegant link between the old and new cities and its current appearance was completed in the 1950s.

75 top The narrow streets of the old Medina, lined with a multitude of houses and workshops, stretch as far as the eye can see to the distant blue horizon of the sea, dominated by the minaret of the Hassan II Mosque.

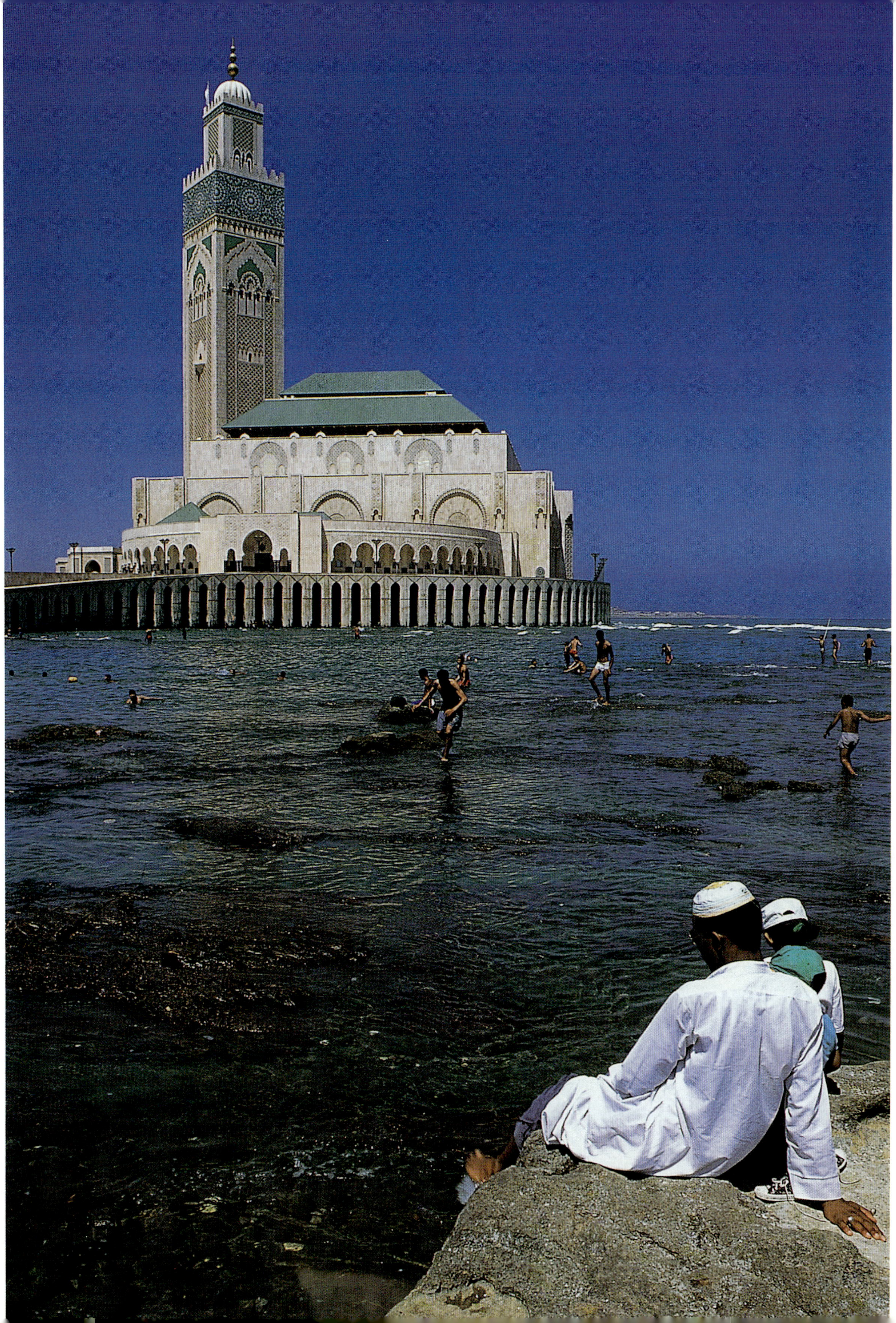

ings that have eroded its 18th century structure so that, today, the narrow streets are more characteristic than beautiful and retain only a token value. They remind the visitor that, behind the rush and the lights, Casablanca hides a more traditional spirit than is apparent. But the city was also the showpiece of the French protectorate; in Boulevard Mohammed V there are many buildings

76 Designed by the French architect, Michel Pinseau, the Hassan II mosque is a magnificent temple that seems to float on the waves of the Atlantic. Begun in 1980, it was completed in thirteen years and financed via national subscription.

77 top left Hassan II mosque can be recognized in this evening view; its minaret also acts as a lighthouse. Standing 689 feet tall and with a base of eighty-two feet square, it has a laser beam that points in the direction of Mecca, Islam's holy city.

77 center left Hassan II mosque was built on the wishes of the king whose name it bears, and is the most dramatic mosque in the Moslem world. It stands on the site of an old municipal swimming pool to the south of Casablanca.

77 bottom left Contrasts of light and shadow inside the mosque emphasize the inlays and ornaments manufactured by Morocco's most skilful craftsmen. In addition to its prayer and ablution rooms, the building contains a library, a museum and an underground garage.

77 top right Granite columns and arches support Hassan II mosque, the third largest and most complex Islamic structure in the world.

77 right bottom Despite its size, the facade of Hassan II mosque is elegant in form. The main entrance is 'lightened' by refined decorations and leads into an architectural complex measuring 968,751 square feet in surface area.

78 bottom A peddlar offers food in a kiosk outside the walls of the old medina. Unlike other Moroccan cities, the buildings in Casablanca are mostly modern. No trace remains of the buildings that were destroyed in the 1755 earthquake.

78-79 and 79 top Spice sellers in Casablanca medina. Moroccan cooking uses generous quantities of spices generally grown in the country.

79 bottom center The neat and brightly colored fruit stalls offer the best Morocco has to offer, produced in the flourishing plantations inland.

79 bottom All sorts of things can be bought in the tiny but densely filled shops in the city center: spices, household items, sweets, traditional cosmetics and so on.

79 top center A chicken seller shows off his produce in the medina. The market in the historical center offers a colorful daily choice of foodstuffs.

in which local architecture is fused with typically Parisian features. On the seafront, however, the visitor is dwarfed by the massive bulk of the Hassan II mosque, the building that the king wanted built to be a symbol of North Africa as the Statue of Liberty is for the United States. Its dimensions speak for themselves: the prayer hall can accommodate 20,000 worshippers and another 80,000 can be held in the square, while a laser beam, visible from twenty-two miles away, shows the direction of Mecca from the 689 feet high minaret. Despite its enormous size, the building is elegantly designed and its interior decorations are beautifully refined. The mosque and Al-Hank lighthouse stand at either end of the Corniche that winds along the seafront lined by cafés and restaurants; it is a favorite place for a stroll and provides lovely views over the sea and the city.

82

82 top left Rabat's flea market brings life to the alleyways that line the city walls. If you are happy to haggle and you know the local crafts, you can find bargains in the form of tea-sets, coins and small items of furniture.

82 top right Avenue Mohammed V is the heart of modern Rabat. Lined with shops, restaurants and cafés, the largest city street connects the old city to the modern, western style districts. Among the buildings on the tree-lined street are the city Post Office, the railway station and the National Bank of Morocco.

82-83 The fish market at the outlet of the Bou Regreg river. Fishing is a principal source of revenue for Morocco with the national waters providing 150,000 tons of sea food every year.

83 top Bab al-Oudaja is the gate that enters the kasbah of the same name; it is one of the most refined works from the Almohad period. Built to be more decorative than defensive, its bulk is decorated with elegant bas-reliefs.

Oudaia Kasbah is one of the country's loveliest forts. The huge and richly embellished Oudaia Gate seems to have been built more for decoration than defense. Inside the fort there are twisting alleys, the Jama al Atiq mosque and a wide terrace on the defensive walls that gives a marvelous view over the Atlantic, the river and the city of Salé opposite.

83 bottom The Bou Regreg river separates the capital from the city of Salé; the two walled historical centers recall the period when local pirates terrorized the Spanish and Portuguese shipping.

Even more impressive in the austere solemnity of its architecture is Hassan's Tower. Built in 1190, it was intended to be the minaret of antiquity's largest mosque but on the death of its benefactor, Yacoub al Mansour, construction of the mosque was abandoned. Today the tower stands in the center of a large esplanade in front of the mausoleum of Mohammed V, the father of modern Morocco, and overlooks an army of columns. Mohammed's mausoleum appears rather somber from the outside but the interior dazzles the eye with more than 10,764 square feet of mosaic. Near Rabat and protected by defensive walls are the remains of the Marinid burial sites at Chellah and the Roman settlement of Sala.

84 top left and bottom right Though the exterior of Mohammed V's mausoleum is essentially simple, the interior astonishes the visitor with its wealth of detail. Each of the 10,764 square feet of mosaic that lines the walls is made using two thousand tiles. A bronze chandelier measuring eight feet in diameter hangs from the ceiling.

84 bottom left A royal guard presides over the mausoleum of Mohammed V, the king who restored Morocco to independence. Inside, prayers are unceasingly recited in honor of the dead king, day and night.

84-85 Hassan Tower is what remains of what must have been the largest mosque in the Islamic world. The square minaret, 144 feet tall, would have reached a final height of 262 feet if it had been completed. The walls are richly decorated with low reliefs and are often over seven feet thick.

85 top The presence of the Bou Regreg river meant that there have been settlements in this area since antiquity. Excavations in Chellah necropolis show that the area was inhabited during the third century BC.

VOTREPENSION
Café Riad
Patisserie Glacier
ALIMENTATION GENERAL

TANGIERS, GATEWAY TO THE WORLD

Greek mythology says that Tangiers was founded by the giant Antaeus, son of Poseidon, lord of the sea, and Gaea, goddess of the earth. It was Antaeus that baptized the city with the name of his wife, Tingi, which in Arabic becomes Tanjah-Tangeri. Through this strategically important port have passed all the peoples that are part of Moroccan history: Berbers, Carthaginians, Romans, Idrisids, Ummayads, Moslems, Portuguese, Spanish, English, Germans and, of course, the French. In 1912, the "Gateway to Africa" was finally considered an international zone to be controlled by a dozen nations and a representative of the sultan.

It is not possible to understand the fascination of Tangiers without knowing the eventful political developments that created this uniquely human city, the most cosmopolitan and tolerant in North Africa and a permanent favorite with artists and writers. Its medina stands on top of a hill that dominates the port. The alleys open onto the Great Mosque and the small Spanish-style square of Petit Socco where colorful markets are held. Forming an ideal connection to the new districts at the exit of the medina stands the Gran Socco, a wide square that houses an immense and permanent market where farmers and pedlars compete for business. Still in the upper section of the city, the ancient sultan's palace is located in the *kasbah*

86 top left Traditional stairways can be seen in this view of Tangiers' medina. Built entirely on a rocky outcrop, the white houses and unmistakable atmosphere bewitched Paul Bowles, Tennessee Williams and Paul Morand.

86 top right The Sultan's Palace, Dar al-Makhzen, was built by Moulay Ismail and enlarged in the 18th-19th centuries. Today it is home to what remains of the royal apartments and the Museum of Moroccan Art.

86-87 Tangiers' railway station stands on a large expanse at the foot of the medina with the port and bus station. A busy center, it has many cafés, restaurants and small hotels.

87 top The Great Mosque in Tangiers is one of the buildings that best reflects the city's tormented history. It was first a Roman temple, then a mosque, and later a Portuguese cathedral. It was reconverted to a mosque by Moulay Ismail who, in this manner, celebrated the departure of the British. The photograph shows the main entrance.

87 bottom The port in Tangiers has always had great strategic and commercial importance due to its position on the Strait of Gibraltar. The current basin was built in 1921 and is protected by a breakwater nearly a mile long.

88 top The square in the Large Souk is the commercial heart of Tangiers. The market attracts descendants of the Berbers in traditional costume, many of whom have the blond hair and blue eyes typical of the Fahciya tribe.

88 left It is not uncommon to come across women in traditional dress in Tangiers. Although it is a very cosmopolitan city, Tangiers is traditional at heart and both the inhabitants and the traders from out of town love to wear traditional costume.

but is now used to house the Museum of Moroccan Art. As one heads down towards the sea, the architecture reflects the city's European presence with elegant houses along Boulevard Pasteur and the Hotel Minzah, built by the French in 1933 for Lord Bute, a Scottish nobleman. The hotel's sumptuous Moorish salons have played host to Winston Churchill, Rita Hayworth and the novelist Paul Bowles whose book *Tea in the Desert* was turned into a film by Italian director Bernardo Bertolucci, part of which was shot in the hotel.

88-89 During the fairs on Sundays and Thursdays, the food stalls in the Large Souk offer an unending variety of goods. The traders are often farmers selling produce from their own land.

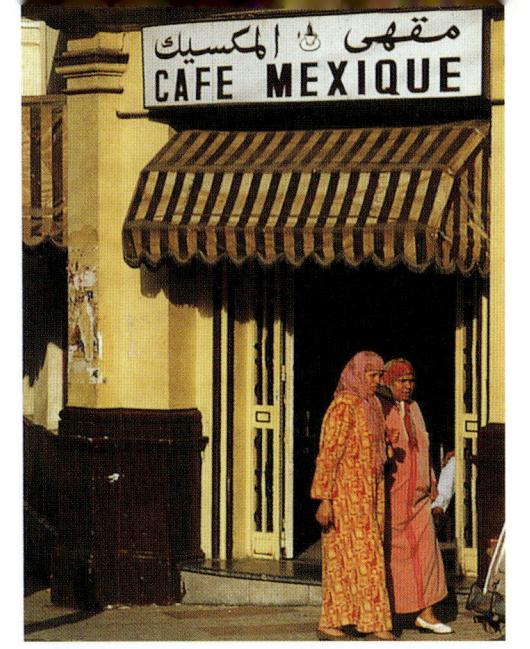

89 top A view of Rue du Mexico in Tangiers where the streets are often named after cities and countries. The exotic place name and local signs in Arabic and French show the true face of Morocco's most international city.

89 center and bottom Souk Dakhil (Small Souk) attracts a busy crowd of sellers and buyers every day. The architecture of the narrow square lined with hotels and cafés is typically Spanish, with finely wrought iron balconies and windows.

90 top Khalifa Palace (the official Royal Palace) was the residence of the Caliph at the time of the protectorate. The building is an example of Hispanic-Moorish architecture from the 17th century but has largely been rebuilt.

90-91 The photograph shows the medina in Tétouan. It contains seventy mosques and is closed on three sides by walls that have seven entrance gates. Its well-preserved buildings date from the end of the 17th century.

TETOUAN, EL JADIDA AND ESSAOUIRA, A HARMONY OF CULTURES

Not far from Tangiers, the city of Tétouan stands on the slopes of Djebel Dersa, one of the most beautiful mountains in the Rif. Local tradition here is solidly intertwined with the presence of the Spanish and has given rise to a unique hybrid architecture that incorporates features of Arab and Andalusian styles. The white streets of the medina, that often lead into small squares, are the best example of this hybrid architecture. The corporations representing crafts and occupations are concentrated in individual streets and it is the colorful "Street of the Dyers" that mostly attracts the interest of the tourists and merchants.

But the coast of Morocco also offers other, though smaller and less frenetic, cities of especial beauty that still display signs of an eventful past. For example, there is Al-Jadida with its austere fort that overlooks the sea, and Essaouira, which used to be famous for its trade in purple dye and sugar. Essaouira is a coastal city with white and blue houses decorated with stylish architectural details; its fortunate situation makes it open to the trade-winds that endow it with a pleasant climate all year round. Its port lies below the bastions of the fort and is filled with a daily spectacle of colored boats and nets laid out in the sun. Always a busy trading city in the past, it is famous for its beautiful and intelligent women – at least the sultans used to think so for they came here to supply their harems.

91 top The largest street in modern Tétouan is Avenue Mohammed V lined with Spanish-style buildings. Wide and elegant, it is the setting for the best hotels, restaurants and shops in the city.

91 center The Portuguese citadel of Al Jadida recalls the 260 years of Portuguese domination of the city. Surrounded by solid walls further strengthened with four bastions, the city was built in the 16th century to the plans of an Italian architect.

91 bottom The water tank built by the Portuguese in 1541 in Al Jadida to catch rainwater is supported by twenty-five columns. Note the cross-vault in late Gothic style.

92 bottom The suggestive backdrop offered by the ramparts in Essaouira was used by Orson Welles for his film Othello, *one of his masterpieces.*

92-93 Essaouira is constantly exposed to the trade winds and, at high tide, the waves often smash against the fortifications. Note the whiteness of the medina behind.

93 top left The fishermen are intently resetting their nets after a day's fishing. Near Essaouira's picturesque and traditional port, there are many small restaurants that cook the day's catch.

93 top right Essaouira is unsurprisingly called the "blue and white city." The streets of its unusually linear medina nearly all have bright blue doors and white walls.

92 top The Skala in Essaouira is a fortified rampart that faces out to sea and offers a splendid view of the old city and the coast. The famous workshops of ebony and cedar carvers – thought to be the best in Morocco – stand at the foot of the wall.

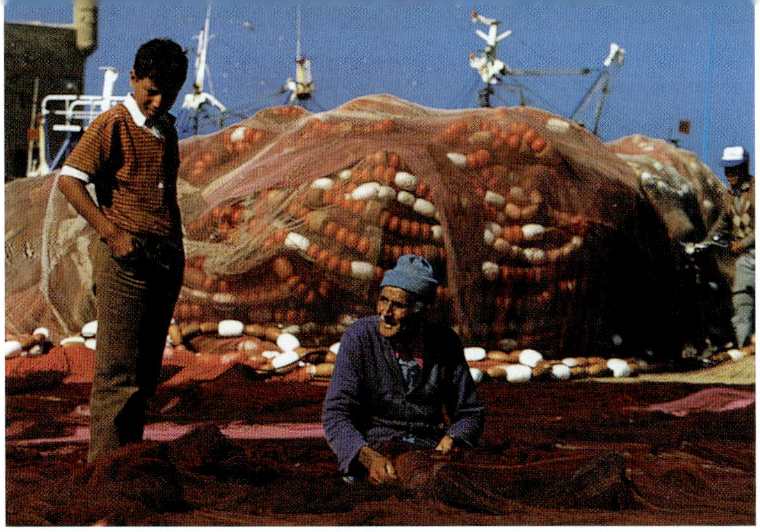

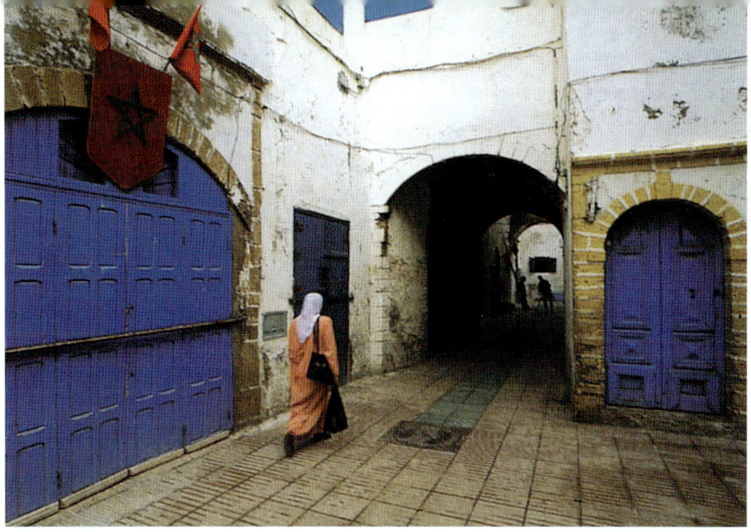

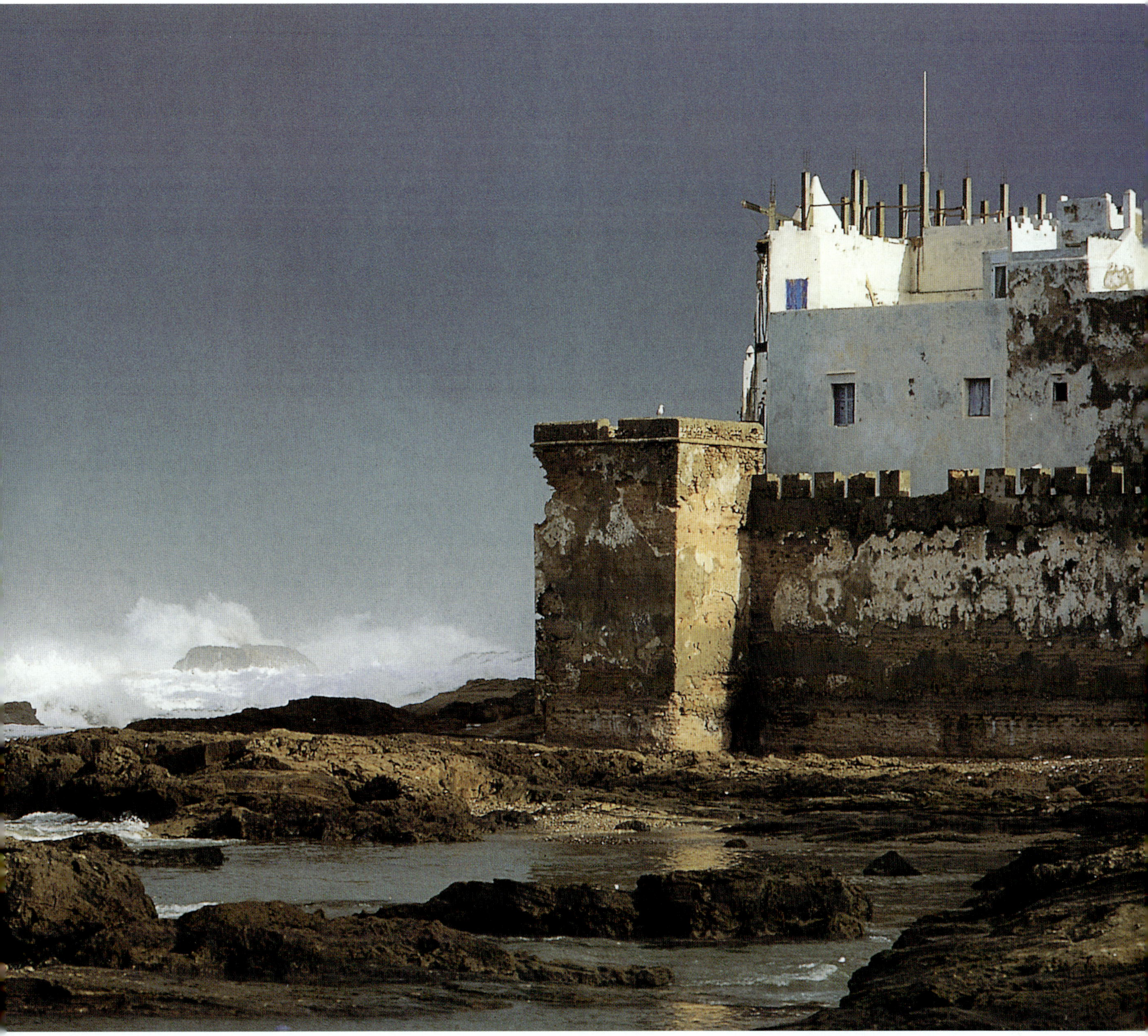

VOLUBILIS, ECHOES OF THE ROMAN EMPIRE

Before turning our attention to the principal cities, Volubilis, the best preserved architectural site in Morocco, should be mentioned. It was one of the largest centers of Mauritania Tingitana and the residence of the Roman procurators that governed the region. It got rich on the trade of olive oil, a business that was so common that one in every four houses in the town had a press. Volubilis did not disappear after the departure of the colonizers but became a Berber city; it lost much of its importance after the foundation of Fez and was abandoned after the catastrophic earthquake of 1755.

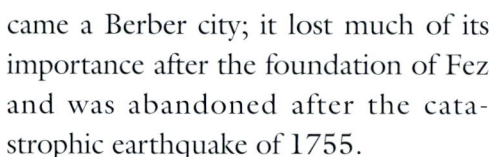

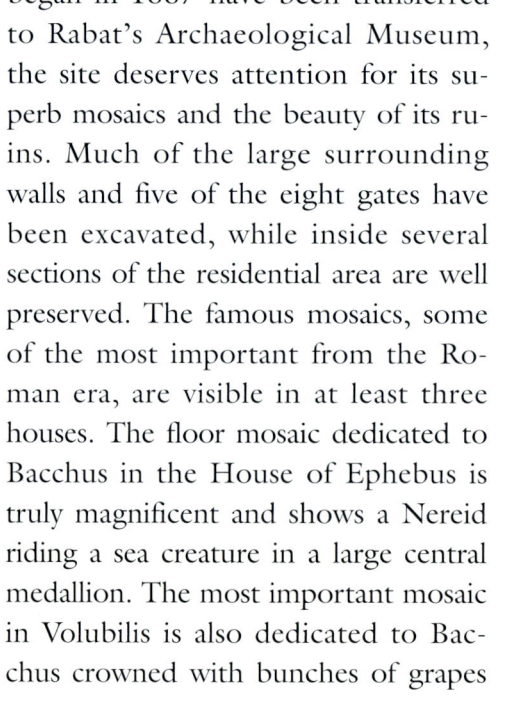

Even though many of the works of art discovered since excavation work began in 1887 have been transferred to Rabat's Archaeological Museum, the site deserves attention for its superb mosaics and the beauty of its ruins. Much of the large surrounding walls and five of the eight gates have been excavated, while inside several sections of the residential area are well preserved. The famous mosaics, some of the most important from the Roman era, are visible in at least three houses. The floor mosaic dedicated to Bacchus in the House of Ephebus is truly magnificent and shows a Nereid riding a sea creature in a large central medallion. The most important mosaic in Volubilis is also dedicated to Bacchus crowned with bunches of grapes

94 center left and bottom The ruins of Volubilis are the most spectacular evidence of the Roman past in Morocco. The site was originally inhabited during the Neolithic period but was then settled by Berber tribes who were vassals of the Phoenicians.

94 top right and 95 top left The Basilica had three naves and two apses. The building was used for different functions: for juridical assemblies and commercial negotiations, and as a meeting place for the city notables.

94

94-95 Caracalla's Triumphal Arch is an elegant structure built in 217 AD on the decumanus maximus *by the Roman prosecutor, Marcus Aurelius Sebastianus, in honor of the emperor and his mother. It was rebuilt in 1933.*

95 top right The front part of the Campidoglio, a large tetrastyle building in Corinthian style. Originally the square it looks onto was surrounded by a wide portico and had an altar in the center.

96 top left The interior of the House of Orpheus which belonged to a rich Romanized Berber family. The wonderful mosaic shows a forest inhabited by wild and domestic animals.

96 top right Fine mosaics from the first half of the third century AD can be seen in the House of Columns. To the left in the image are the two elegant spiral columns with Corinthian capitals.

96-97 The House of the Train of Venus was undoubtedly one of the most elegant in all Volubilis. Many magnificent mosaics can still be seen here; the one in the image shows Diana with nymphs.

and is to be seen in the *House of the Train of Venus* but there are very many other exceptional works, nearly all of mythological scenes: for example, the *Labors of Hercules*, the *Myth of Orpheus* and medallions depicting the *Gorgons*, *Silenus* and the *Four Seasons*. Around these masterpieces stand the remains of columns, streets, arches and temples, all pervaded by a solemnity that reassures the spirit, and set in a green valley cooled by a gentle breeze. It is a setting worthy of such an important historical site.

A few miles from Volubilis stands Moulay Idris, the "holy city" named after the descendant of the Prophet that founded the Idrisid dynasty. He was the first great Moslem ruler of Morocco and is still the most popular *marabout* (holy man) in the country.

97 top right The House of Bacchus and the House of the Four Seasons, both also on the decumanus maximus, *are also two of the most luxurious houses in the city. The mosaic floor of one of the rooms has eight medallions in busts of eight gods.*

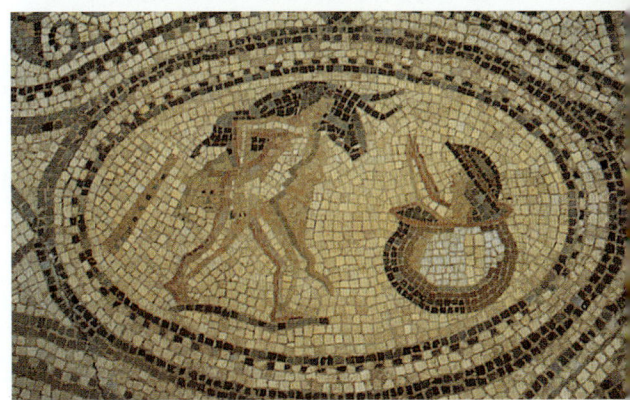

97 bottom left and right The House of Hercules is named after the mosaics of the mythological god. In the two medallions shown, Hercules is portrayed strangling the serpents and fighting the Minotaur.

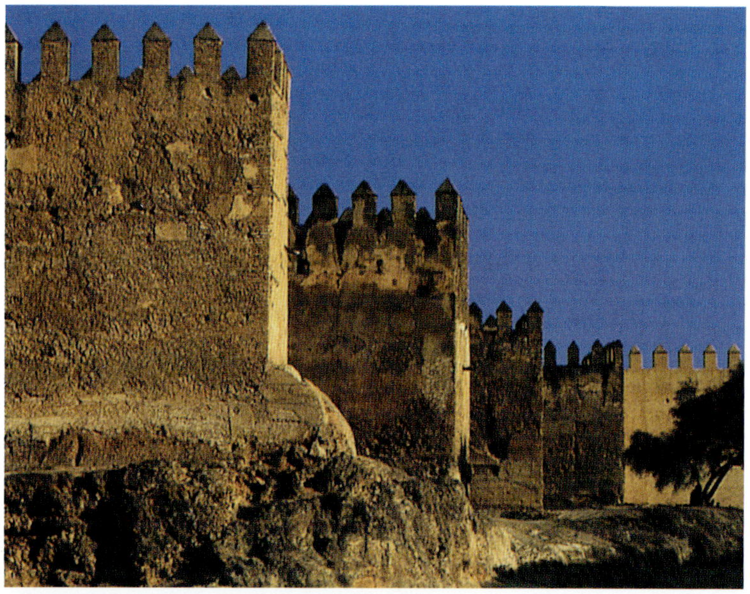

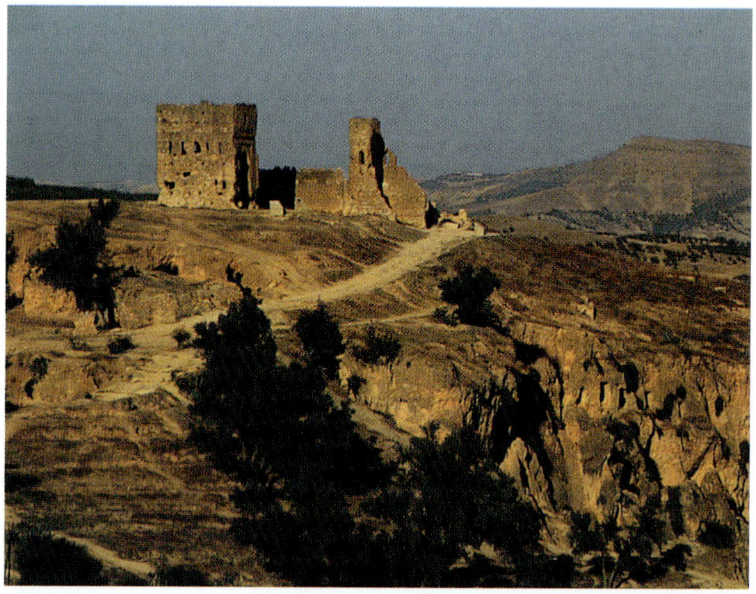

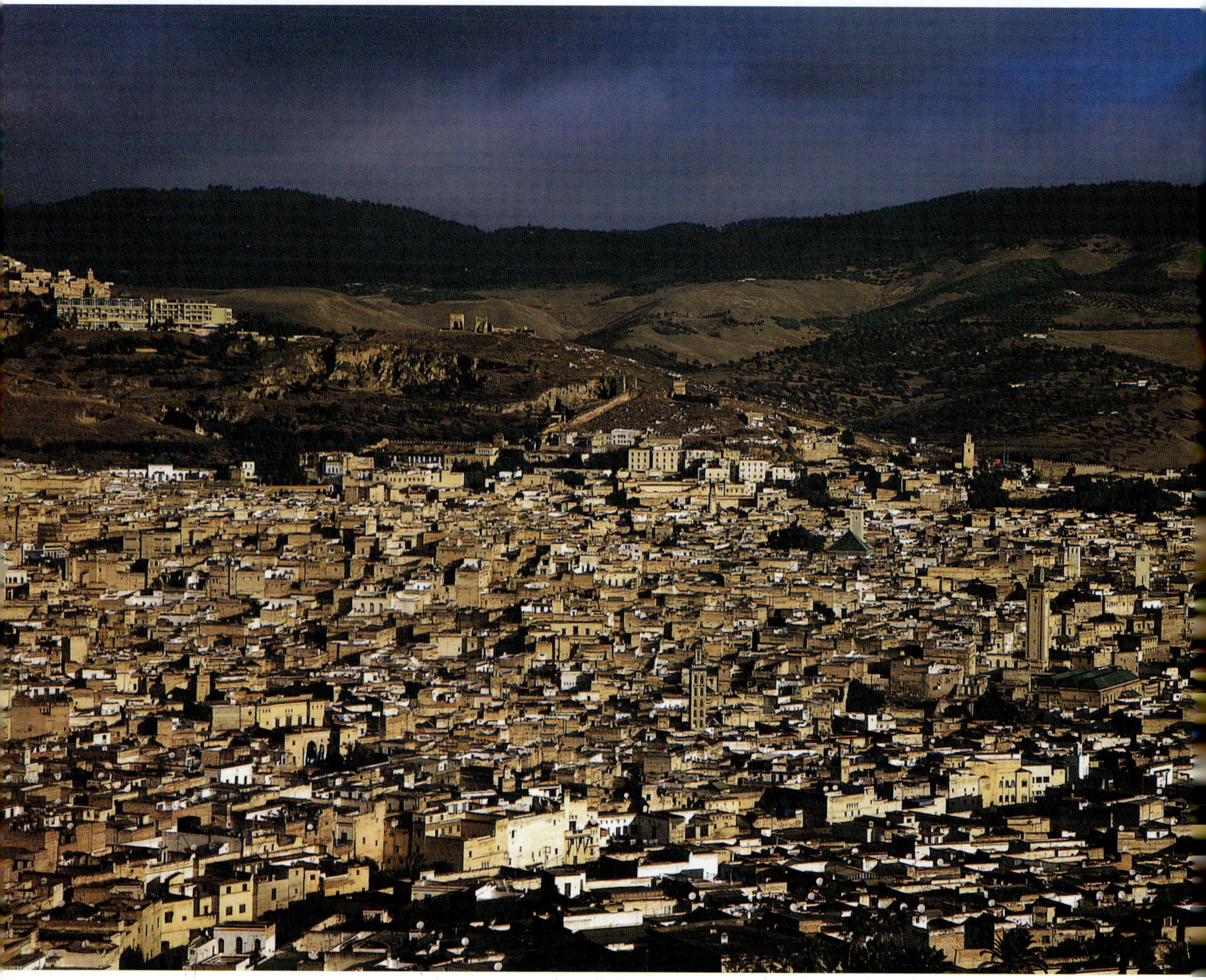

FEZ, THE TREASURE OF THE EMPIRE

99 top The entrance to Fez medina is one of the most beautiful in the Islamic world. It is impossible not to be enchanted by the tangle of alleys where use of the car is prohibited; packed with people, the medina is also the location of unequalled artistic treasures.

99 bottom Detail of the decorations in the medersa al-Attarin, built from 1323-25. One of the masterpieces of Marinid art, the elegant interior of the building is just the prelude to the breathtaking view seen from the terrace.

Idris I was the founder of Fez, the oldest of Morocco's imperial cities and the most important in the country from an artistic and historical viewpoint. Set in the plain of Oued, it is divided into three large districts: Fez al Bali and Fez al Jedid make up the large old center, and the Ville Nouvelle was built by the French starting in 1916. It was the first Islamic city in Morocco and is traditionally less strongly tied to Berber traditions. Since 791, Fez was the preferred destination of Arabs arriving from elsewhere in North Africa, of Andalusian Arabs and, finally, of refugees from Tunisia.

Throughout the vicissitudes of the various Moroccan dynasties, Fez has always been an important cultural center. Its artistic and political peak was reached during the 14th century with the Marinid dynasty. Boasting palaces and *medersa* (Koranic schools) of great beauty, Fez became the capital of a powerful and respected empire the aim of which was the Islamicization of all of northern Africa starting from the west.

This was the period during which Fez al Jedid was built, the quarter that separates the old city from the new, French district. Fez al Jedid is the home of the imperial palace Dar el Makhzen and the Jewish district, Mellah. The first, where the sover-

98 top left The nine miles long walls of Fez encircle the two centers of the old city, Fez al-Jedid and Fez al-Bali. The original walls were built during the Almohad dynasty while the layout of the city buildings has been altered many times over the centuries.

98 top right The necropolis of the Marinid sultans was built in the 14th century; only the walls and a few ruins remain of the ancient buildings, originally of great splendor. In recompense, there is a superb view over the whole of the city.

98-99 The fort of Bordj South gives a marvelous view over the city of Fez. The bastion in the southern section of the city walls was built by Christian prisoners in the 17th century.

100 top left and 101 right The medersa *Bou Inania is a treasure house of ornamental decoration. The photographs show a detail of the entrance, finely carved in cedarwood, and one of the many plaster calligraphic decorations. Built in the mid-14th century, the medersa was the last of the great Marinid buildings in Fez.*

100 centre left Kairaouine mosque seen from above with its lovely cloister is the most popular religious building in the city as well as being one of the oldest universities in the Moslem world. It was founded in 859 by Fatima, has a surface area of 172,222 square feet and can accommodate 22,000 worshippers.

eign still stays, has an elegant ivory colored facade, superb gilded doors and lovely pine-green Saracen roof tiles. The Jewish quarter is the Islamic version of European ghettos; a series of restrictions were imposed upon the inhabitants, for example, when leaving the ghetto, they could not wear shoes or boots, nor could they ride animals. On the other hand, it is said that the Jews had an important constitutional task to perform: that of salting the heads of enemies displayed on the city gates! This was the origin of the name Mellah as *melh* means salt. Inside the quarter, which used to be shut up every evening, the visitor can see elegant grated windows and wooden balconies inlaid with wrought iron decorations on houses that used to belong to the better off Jewish merchants.

Entering Fez al Bali, the ancient medina, is like entering another world. It is the oldest section of the city and certainly the most beautiful. Its charm is unique and overwhelms the visitor on each occasion. Certified as a World Heritage site by UNESCO, it is formed by two quarters, al-Kairaouine and al-Andalous surrounded by a defensive wall. Inside, the street layout is incredibly intricate and after entering one of the gateways, beyond which it is only possible to travel on foot, one loses one's sense of direction almost immediately. The amazingly narrow streets take unexpected turns and it is easy to find oneself back where one began or get lost completely.

100 bottom left Religious prohibitions mean that only a small part of the Moulay Idriss zaouia can be visited. Access to the room in which the remains of the ruler are laid out is also forbidden to Moslem women.

100 top right The Marinid dynasty built many palaces in Fez medina. Built between the 13th and 15th centuries with simple and sometimes modest facades, they are decorated with stuccoes, chased bronze works and columns of great beauty inside and in the internal courtyards.

101 left Moulay Idriss zaouia is the city's religious heart. Prohibited to non-Moslems, it is the destination of daily pilgrimages by the faithful. It was built at the start of the tenth century and completely rebuilt in 1437.

101

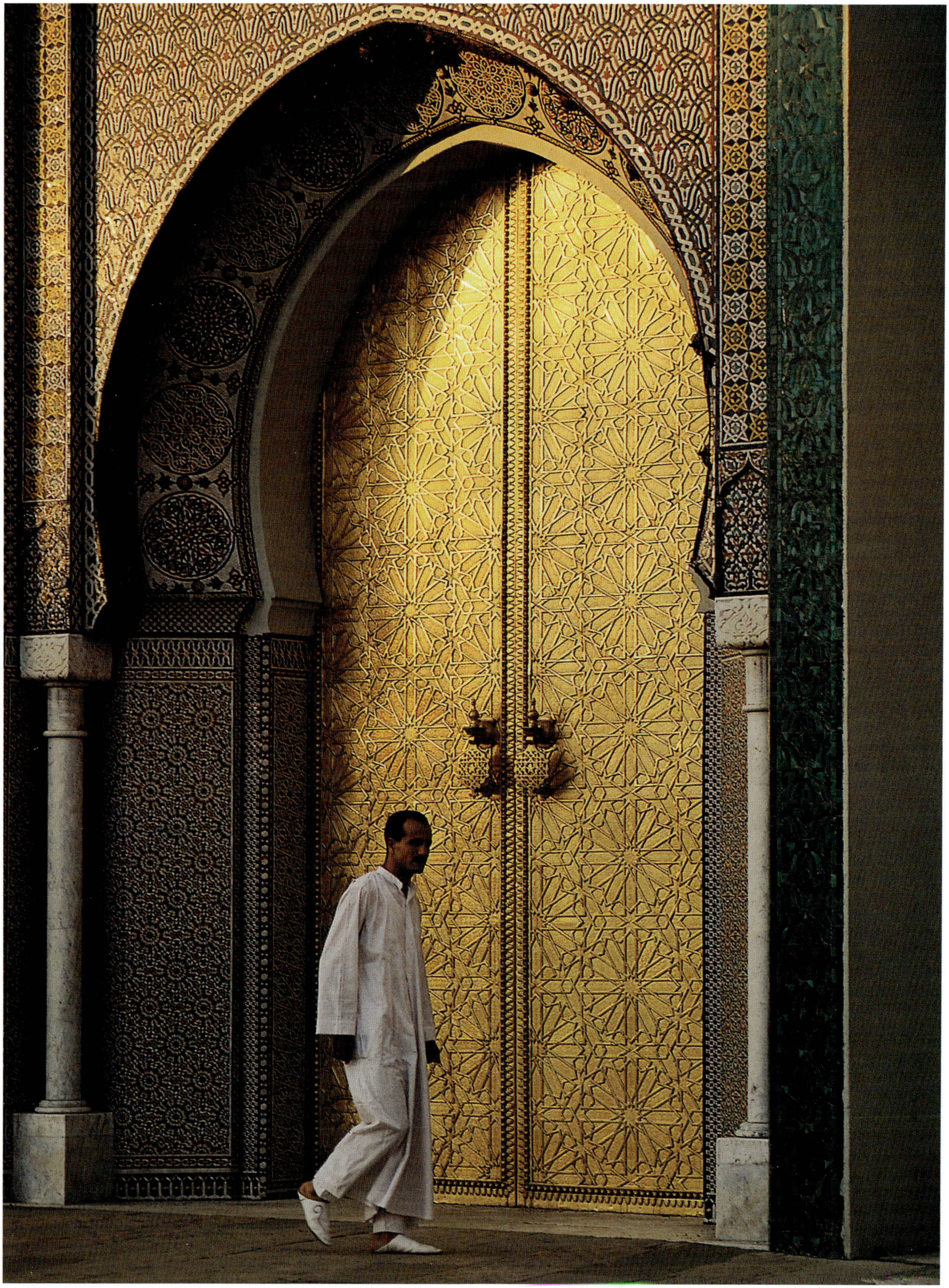

102 and 103 top left The beautiful Royal Palace (Dar al-Makhzen) keeps its superb portals closed to all but the royal family and its retinue. The building overlooks the modern Place des Alouites and was built at the start of the 20th century. In the past, this part of the palace was hidden by a protective wall but the wall was knocked down to give a better view of the building's lovely facade.

the logical result of a medieval Islamic city governed by precise religious and town-planning regulations which were dominated by commerce. Fate has preserved this world in one piece to the modern day in one of its most perfect examples. The number of architectural treasures in this part of the city is surprising: the *medersa* Bou Inania is a masterpiece of decoration and calligraphic art in marble, wood, glass,

103 bottom right The medersa *Bou Inania is an old and famous Koranic school decorated with onyx and marble tiles. The buildings once used by students and teachers for prayer face onto the internal courtyard.*

This confusing ambience is the starting point of the magic of the medina, a labyrinth in which one is assaulted by smells, colors and voices. It is a labyrinth in which beautiful buildings unexpectedly appear in front of you as if the architect had acted upon his inspiration without caring about the location. Although it seems a state of pure architectural anarchy, that is not really the case. The medina is

103 bottom left The courtyard of the 18th century en-Nejjarin fondouk. It has three orders of galleries that look outwards. Most of the doors give access to the storerooms where traders kept spices and imported goods.

106 top left The Royal Palace in Meknès is a huge complex built in several phases that is so large it seems like a complete district. The first buildings date from the 17th century and, since then, each ruler has indulged in restorations and additions.

106 center left The external decorations on the Great Mosque are as delicate as embroidery and give the building a sumptuous and magical appearance. Two hundred years after its construction, the building was enlarged and embellished in the domes and internal areas.

106 bottom left The elegant decorations around the windows of medersa *Bou Inania* are in Hispanic-Moorish style. Built by the Marinid sultans Abou al-Hassan and Abau Inan, the complex is famous for its enameled majolica mosaics and plaster sculptures.

106 bottom right One of the richly decorated doors of the Great Mosque, one of the city's most popular places of worship. Built in the 12th century, it seems inspired by Mohamed's house of exile in Medina in Saudi Arabia.

106-107 The decorations on the main gate of the Royal Palace in Meknès were restored during the 19th century. As with the rest of the royal palaces, it is only possible for common mortals to walk around the outer walls.

MEKNES, THE DREAM OF MOULAY ISMAIL

At the foot of the extreme northern tip of the Middle Atlas not far from Fez, stands Meknes, the 17th century imperial dream of the Almoravid dynasty that was turned into one of Morocco's most beautiful cities by Moulay Ismail making use of more than 30,000 slaves. Today it is divided by the river Oued Boufekrane: to the east lie the modern districts built during the last few decades, and to the west is the medina and the Imperial City with its artistic jewels. It is ringed by twenty-five miles of defensive walls in three orders in which a series of monumental gateways give access to the city: Bab al-Bardayn, Bab al-Khémis and the beautiful Bab al-Mansour.

106

107 top left Bab al-Mansour is unquestionably the loveliest and most impressive gateway to the city. Facing the square, the facade is decorated with marvelous low reliefs and colored mosaics. At one time, the decapitated heads of those that suffered the death penalty were hung outside the gate.

107 top right The emerald green roofs and minaret of the medersa Bou Inania. The building was built on the traditional plan of Koranic schools with a large central courtyard onto which the student accommodations and a gallery faced on three sides.

114

114 top left and top right Completely renovated in 1986, the Mamounia Hotel is considered one of the top hotels in the world. Surrounded by thirteen hectares of grounds, it was a favorite of Winston Churchill who considered it a perfect spot to indulge in his hobby of painting. The building was named after Mamoun, the son of Sultan Sidi Mohammed.

mosque the large facade of which features denticulated merlons. The necropolis contains the sarcophagi of the thirteen rulers of the Sa'di dynasty. The delicacy of the decoration and the harmony of the overall design make it a masterpiece of funerary art.

Another of Marrakesh's most sumptuous buildings is also one of the more recent, the Mamounia Hotel. Dating only from 1923, its splendor seems much older and its guest book contains such famous names as Winston Churchill, Rita Hayworth, Orson Welles and Richard Nixon. But the city's real heart beats in the lively *souks*, the heirs of an extraordinary commercial past, and in the central Place Jemaa

114-115 The large court of medersa *Ali bin Youssef has a central pool for ablutions. The decorated arches, the* zellij *(ceramic) plinth and plaster ornaments are all of fine quality.*

115 bottom left Prayer hall in medersa *Ali bin Youssef, the largest Koranic school in the Maghreb. Note the marble columns whose decorations refer to the origins and glory of the founder.*

115 top right The tombs of the Sa'di rulers were built from 1590-1600 and later walled in by Moulay Ismail who wanted to hide every trace of the dynasty. It was only in 1917 that the two mausoleums in the necropolis were revealed.

115 bottom right The interiors of the Sa'di tombs are decorated with mosaics, frescoes and inlays of cedar wood. They hold the remains of four sultans and sixty-two members of the royal family.

116 top left The kiosks in Place Jemaa al-Fna offer the most popular dishes in Moroccan cooking which are generally eaten standing. The smoke of the cooking covers the square with a cloud of spicy aromas.

116 center left Marrakesh souk is the largest in the country and the visitor will be confounded by the variety of goods displayed in the mesh of alleyways. The market contains the best of Moroccan crafts, jewelry and foodstuffs.

al-Fna. The square is both a meeting and transit point for merchants and farmers and is in continuous ferment which rises to fever pitch each afternoon and evening. This is not just a market for buying and selling, it is also a place of entertainment; it is the stage for street musicians, healers, jugglers and story-tellers.

Just a little outside the city in the new residential zone lie the Menara gardens. These are a haven of coolness and tranquillity watered by a large artificial pool built by the Almohads.

116 bottom left An olive seller shows his wares in large bottles and traditional earthenware pots. The food market in Marrakesh has been the best stocked for centuries as the city's strategic position has always made it a trading center.

116 bottom right Many family run workshops dye fabrics in the Souk-aux-Teinturiers. The techniques used are still the traditional ones, handed down through the generations.

116-117 Place Jemaa al-Fna is the unquestioned heart of the city where each evening provides a large, open air spectacle. Dozens of small cafés and restaurants offer music and food while artists, pedlars and fire-eaters display themselves and their wares.

117 top The large pool in Menara Park was built in the 12th century for the sultans of the Almohad dynasty. The pool is surrounded by an enormous garden that is mostly used for growing olives.

CHECHAOUEN, THE SPIRIT OF ANDALUSIA

118 bottom The Andalusian-style park of the kasbah *in Chechaouen has grounds offering peace and serenity which contrast with the knowledge that the plain buildings that surround them were used as a prison.*

118-119 Chechaouen benefits from its enviable geographical position which has meant that it has been less affected than most Moroccan cities by invasions and European influences. Note the dazzling whiteness of the medina.

119 top left and top center Two views of the elegant Place Outa al-Hammam from which the red walls of the kasbah *rise. Once the heart of a "forbidden city," it is now open to visitors and its palaces have been turned into small hotels, restaurants and cafés.*

119 right Traditional houses in Chechaouen medina combine plaster white with light blue or mauve tones. These Andalusian-style houses are often decorated with wrought iron balconies, large carved doors and skilfully shaped mouldings. The cobbles of the narrow sloping streets heighten the beauty of the city's unspoiled historical center.

So far we have discussed the country's major cities, the ones that are impossible to ignore, but deeper exploration will bring other, interesting surprises. To the north, sheltered by the peaks of Djebel Kalaa and Djebel Meggou, lies Chechaouen, founded in 1471 by Andalusian exiles. Strongly tied to Islam, the city has always proudly resisted the incursions of European civilization and was, until 1920, "prohibited" to non-Moslems. The people like to say that the many local springs were a gift from Allah to the city's inhabitants and, in fact, the fertility of the valley has always encouraged agriculture and commerce. The city's lovely medina with its houses with blue and white roofs is a warren of alleyways that dominates the surrounding countryside. The focus of the historical center is the tree and café-lined Place Outa al-Hammam which forms the heart of city life. In a small park far from the center stands the Moulay Ali bin Rachid mosque, a funerary building in memory of the city's founder, the *sharif* that built Chechaouen to prevent the invasion of Morocco by the Spanish and Portuguese.

119

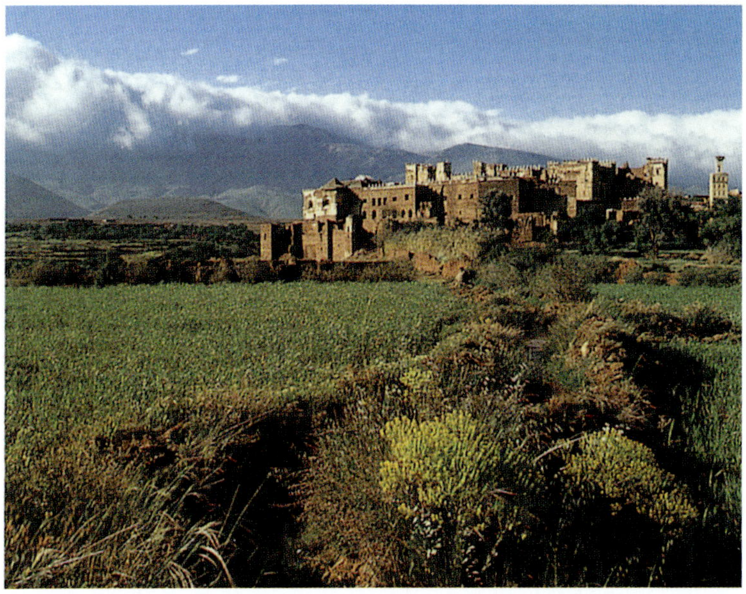
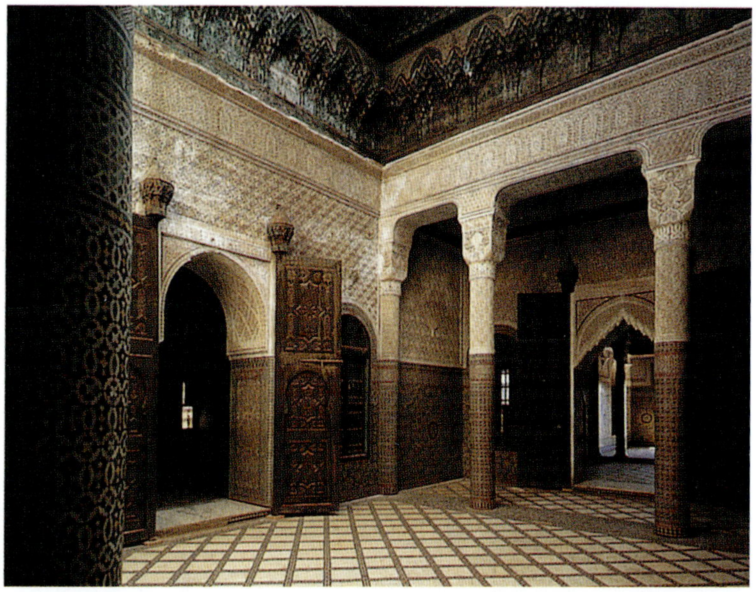
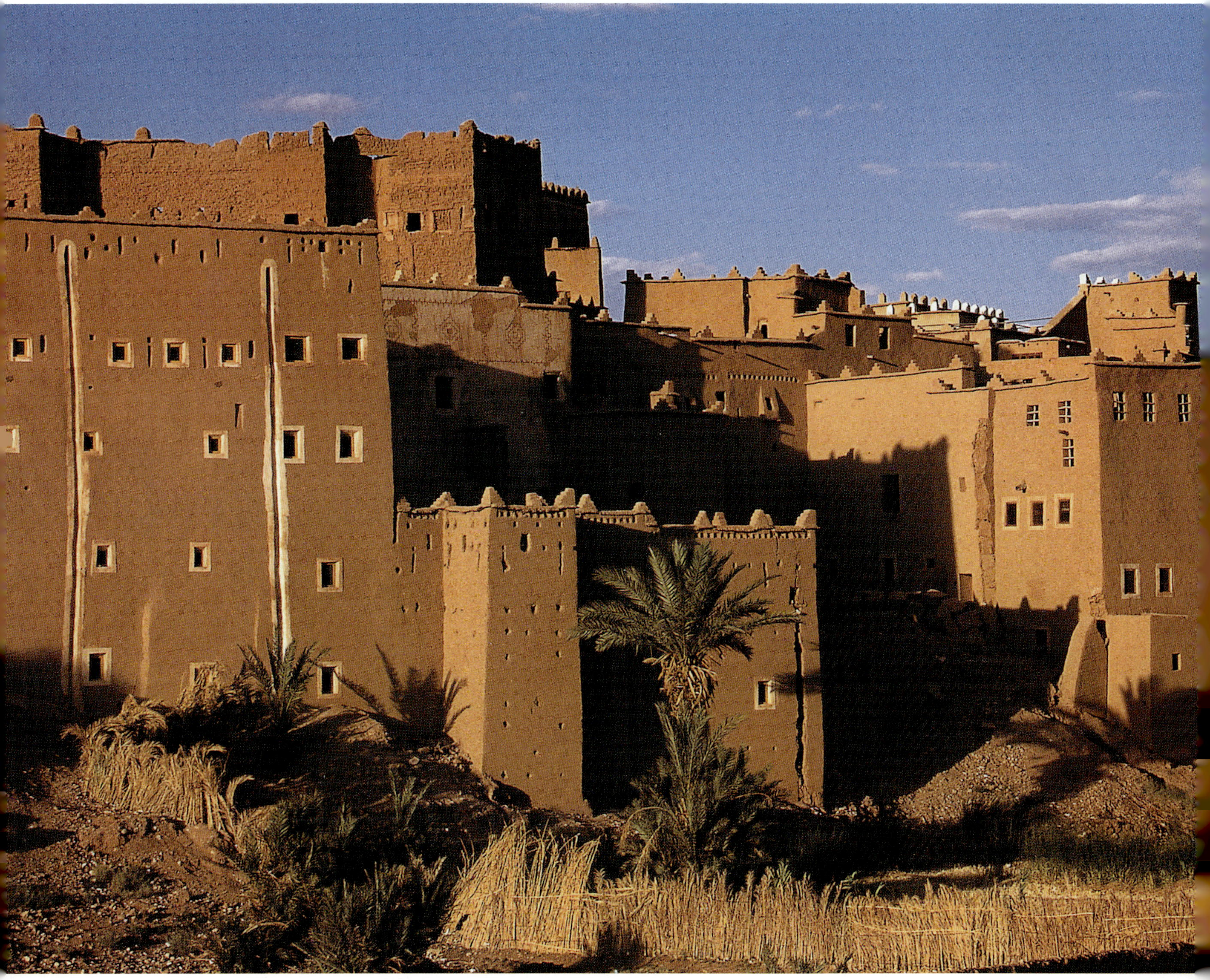

OUARZAZATE, TELOUET E AGADIR BETWEEN DESERT AND SEA

120 top left The 19th century kasbah of Télouet rises against the sky in the High Atlas. At one time, the kasbah was home to a thousand or so people; it was a fort of great strategic importance that supported the local autonomous political power.

120 top right Only two rooms remain of the elegant interiors of Thami al-Glaoui kasbah. Stuccoes, wall decorations similar to fabrics and painted ceilings recall the elegant Andalusian style that characterized the whole complex.

120-121 The large Taourirt kasbah in Ouarzazate was built of mud and earth but it is certainly one of the most attractive in Morocco. The rich apartments inside are in good condition; folkloristic events are held in the courtyard.

Apart from Marrakesh, the south of the country offers other marvelous sights, perhaps less well-known but of equal appeal. Ouarzazate has a modern exterior but a traditional heart. It stands on a plateau on the borders of the Sahara where it was founded in 1928 by the Foreign Legion. A mile or so from the center you will find the austere solemnity of the Taourirt kasbah where scenes from Bertolucci's film *Tea in the Desert* was filmed.

Télouet lies in the same region dominated by its Berber kasbah that has, unfortunately, been only partly restored. Both a fort and a village, the complex of buildings still retains decorations, capitals and ceilings of great refinement that commemorate a strong local power, the Caid of Glaoua, who benefited from the strategic importance of the area. With the agreement of the French, the lords of Télouet still controlled large swathes of south Morocco at the start of the last century.

Further south, but on the Atlantic coast, Agadir takes the visitor into another realm altogether. The immense beach and the large international hotels offer tourists a typical western beach holiday. The city's old section was destroyed completely during a tremendous earthquake in 1960 and reconstruction of Agadir was made to incorporate anti-seismic measures. The ancient city may have disappeared for good, but the new buildings have contributed to the expansion of coastal tourism. Today Agadir represents the most modern and commercial side of a great empire whose soul is rooted in the past.

121 top Most of Agadir's hotels are to be found strung out along the bay. The city's night life is typical of international tourist resorts.

121 bottom The beach facilities in Agadir bay belong to the hotels which together offer a total of 17,000 beds.

124 bottom left and top right Tuareg women traditionally wear blue and indigo clothes and are famous for their beauty. Tall and slim, and with a regal bearing, their mystery has attracted generations of western writers who have included them in travel accounts and stories.

124-125 A group of Tuareg watch a festival being held in an oasis from a rock. The most important moussem of the Reguibat tribe is held at the beginning of June every year at Goulimine.

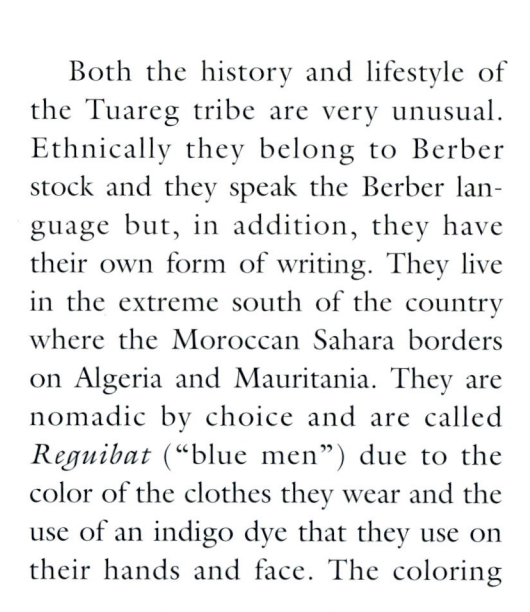

Both the history and lifestyle of the Tuareg tribe are very unusual. Ethnically they belong to Berber stock and they speak the Berber language but, in addition, they have their own form of writing. They live in the extreme south of the country where the Moroccan Sahara borders on Algeria and Mauritania. They are nomadic by choice and are called *Reguibat* ("blue men") due to the color of the clothes they wear and the use of an indigo dye that they use on their hands and face. The coloring has a double purpose: it is used as a protection against the sun, the wind and insects on the exposed parts of the body, and also to ward off evil spirits and misfortune.

The Tuareg live in close harmony with their wild and difficult environment whose every nuance they are familiar with. The sand and silence of the Sahara have consolidated their fiery rebellious spirit that loathes any kind of rule or restriction. Bandits and merchants on the desert caravan routes, their lives are seriously threatened by modern life. Now that the era of the great caravans is past and trade by camel is in decline, they have also been hemmed in by the interminable conflict between Morocco and the Polisario Front. In a world that seems to rule their future out, they are still able to meet, as solemn as ever, in the famous market at Goulimine, the last outpost for their dignified form of trading. They have no intention of surrendering to modern civilization; they are the last poets of the desert, proud of their ancient heritage that no empire has ever succeeded in taming.

The status of women is higher among the Berber than in the Islamic world; there is no obligation to wear the veil, polygamy is not practiced and women have a substantial influence on clan decisions. Their religion is Islam although several ancient rites are still practiced by tribes furthest away from the cities.

125 top The "blue men" find their natural habitat among the infinite dunes of Merzouga. Now reduced to just a few thousand, this people of Berber origin impress with their capacity to maintain their traditional lifestyle.

126 top Berber music is based on the heavy use of drums whose style differs with the area. Wind instruments are secondary in importance and provide simple accompaniment to the rhythm of the drums.

126-127 Dance is an essential component of traditional Moroccan festivals which are mostly based on Berber customs. The most common form of the dance is when the men and women dance in a circle around the musicians.

The common Islamic religion and unions between the main ethnic groups make Morocco a nation that happily tolerates co-existence of different cultures.

The mother-tongue of almost half the population of Morocco is Arabic and Arab culture dominates the country. The people, however, are not a single ethnic group, being mostly descended from the original Berber stock that adopted Arab customs after the two groups mixed. Most of the Arabs live along the coast, in the plains and the in area of the Sahara; perhaps unexpectedly, there is a strong strain of Andalusian blood within the Moroccan Arab community that came from the *moriscos* who were chased out of Spain by the Catholic monarchs during the period 1492-1614. The original influx of Arabs occurred with the arrival of nomad tribes during the first expansion of Islam towards north-west Africa at the beginning of the eight century and the people descended from this wave still inhabit the Saharan section of the country.

Other ethnic populations are Aratini and Jews. The first are black Africans who arrived in the south of Morocco as slaves during the Sa'di dynasty of Moulay Ismail. Although they occupy a low position on the social scale, they are respected for their presumed magical and miraculous powers. They are evident in the markets of the south of the country, especially Marrakesh, where they sing, dance and perform propitiatory rites in public.

The Jews were once a large community but are now just a tiny minority. They have been present in Morocco since 70 AD when they fled Palestine after the destruction of Solomon's Temple in Jerusalem.

Morocco's rich folklore is derived from both Arab and Berber elements. Classical Andalusian music has traditional centers in Fez, Tétouan and Rabat and uses instruments from around the Mediterranean such as the lute, mandolin and flute. Berber music, on the other hand, is more percussive and based on sensual

127 top The moussem at Fez celebrates the figure of Moulay Ismail II, the founder of the city. The most popular festival of the year, it follows the Islamic calendar and is held at the end of August or in early September.

127 center and bottom Covering one's head is a common tradition for men and women throughout the Moslem Maghreb. It is not just religious in nature but also beneficial for reasons of hygiene and the environment. White cotton cloths protect the head from the sun and wind and prevent the sand from entering.

rhythms that are suitable for choreographic body movement and dances. Traditional instruments accompany the many Moroccan festivals of which there are basically four types: Islamic festivals based on the religious calendar; family festivals; *moussems* (regional celebrations in honor of local *marabout* or holy men); and local lay festivals linked to historical events or to harvest time.

The most important religious festivals are Ramadan, during which Moslems fast by day and party at night-time, the First Moharrem which

Place Mohammed V, 74, 74c, 75c
Place Outa al-Hammam, 118c, 119
Place Zallara, 74c
Plateau des Lacs, 55
Polisario Front, 44, 45c, 124
Polo, Marco, 29
Portuguese citadel, 91c
Poseidon, 87
Ptolemy, 25
Ptolemy, geographer, 31c

R
Rabat, 8, 13, 29, 34, 39c, 42c, 43c, 45c, 51, 80-85, 127
Rasfai, 129
Reguibat, 73c, 124, 124c
Rheriss, 65c, 67c
Ribat, 29
Rif, 40c, 41, 46, 52, 52c, 91, 122
Rio de Oro, 43
Rome, Empire of, 23
Royal Palace in Fez, 3c
Royal Palace in Marrakesh, 112c
Royal Palace in Meknès, 106c
Royal Palace in Rabat, 80, 80c
Rua, 109c
Rue de Mexico, 89c
Rusadir, see Melilla

S
Sa'di, 32, 34, 35c, 110
Safi, 47c
Sahara Desert, 8, 12, 12c, 20, 22, 29, 32, 40c, 43, 45c, 46, 73, 73c, 121, 123c, 124, 124c
Sahrawi, 44
Saint-Exupéry, 13, 48c
Sala, 25, 84
Salé, 34, 80c, 83, 83c, 129

Salvatores, Gabriele, 13
Sanhadja, 29
Sebastian I of Portugal, 32c
Sebou, 55
Senegal, river, 29
Sidi Mohammed, see Mohammed VI
Sidi Mohammed bin Abdallah, 35, 36
Silenus, mosaic of, 97
Skala in Essaouira, 92c
Songai, 32
Souk aux Teinturiers, 116c
Souk Dakhil, 87, 89c
Sous, river, 51, 60c, 65, 122
Stimmer, Tobias, 32c

T
Tafraout, 60c, 62c
Tafrout, 65
Tahar bin Jelloun, 45
Tamrhakht, 49c
Tamuda, 11, 25
Tangiers, 8, 13, 25, 31, 31c, 35, 39, 46c, 48, 86-89, 91
Tanjah-Tangeri, see Tingi
Taourit, 11c
Tarfaya, 48c
Tarhazout, 49c
Tariq Ibn Ziyad, 26, 27c
Taroudannt, 60c
Taza, 29
Télouet, 121
Tétouan, 39, 52, 91, 91c, 127
Timbuktu, 32, 110
Tin Mal, 29
Tingi, 87
Tingis, see Tangiers
Tisouka, 52c
Tizi N'Tichka, 56c, 58c

Tiznit, 51, 51c, 65
Todra, 65c
Tolba, 129
Tessaout Plateau, 60c
Toubkal, 56c
Toubkal massif, 8
Trajan Column, 22c
Treaty of Madrid, 36
Tuareg, 12c, 32

U
Ummayads, 12c, 28
Ussi, Stefano, 37c

V
Valley of the Roses, 11c
Vandals, 26
Vichy regime, 42
Ville Nouvelle, 99
Vo Toan, 80c
Volubilis, 11, 23c, 24c, 25, 94-97

W
Wadi Massa, 49c, 51
Wattasids, 32
Welles, Orson, 92c, 115
Wifaq, 44
Williams, Tennessee, 13, 39, 87c

Y
Yacoub al-Mansour, 29, 84
Youssef bin Tachfin, 29

Z
Zagora, 62c
Zanaga, 122
Zenata, State of, 26
Ziz, 67c

136 Calligraphic and ornamental decorations on the walls of internal courtyards are a lovely example of the Andalusian style wanted by Sultan Moulay Abdallah. Stucco, marble and cedarwood were widely used in the ornamental part of the medersa in the harmonious 16th century works by the area's most skillful craftsmen.

Map Elisabetta Ferrero

PHOTOGRAPHIC CREDITS

AKG Photo: pages 2-7, 20-21, 23 bottom right, 24, 25, 27 bottom right, 33 top, 38, 39 center right, 40-41, 42 top.
AISA: pages 28 top right, 29, 43 bottom.
Stefano Amantini / Atlantide: pages 100 left bottom, 113 top.
Associated Press Photo: pages 40 top, 41 top, 42 bottom, 43 top and center, 44 top, 44-45, 45 top.
Antonio Attini / White Star Archive: pages 74 left center, 94 left center and bottom, 94-95, 95, 96 top right and left, 96-97, 97 bottom left and right.
Louis Audobert / SCOPE: page 60 left bottom.
Bruno Barbier / Hémisphères: pages 59 top right, 104 top.
Tristan Blaise / VISA: pages 55 right bottom, 124 right top.
Christophe Boisvieux: pages 8-9, 9 top right, 20, 48-49, 54, 56 left bottom, 63 top, 64 top right, 67/70, 71, 72 top left, 73, 102, 103 left bottom, 104 bottom, 112 top, 117 top, 127 top, 127 center.
J. Bravo / Ag. Franca Speranza: pages 46 bottom left, 52 top, 123 top right.
British Museum London / The Bridgeman Art Library: page 30 bottom left.
Mark Buscail: pages 56-57.
Stefano Cellai: pages 65 right bottom, 120-121, 130 bottom.
J. Chaves / The Bridgeman Art Library: pages 36-37.
C. Cocchia / Panda Photo: pages 124 left bottom, 124-125.
Private Collection / The Bridgeman Art Library: page 33 center.
Harry Dalton / Jacana: page 56 left top.
Pascale Desclos / SCOPE: pages 64 top left, 129 bottom.
Jean-Léo Dugast / Photobank: pages 66, 91 right bottom.
Double's: pages 22, 30-31, 31 right.
E.T. Archive: page 37 bottom.
Mary Evans Picture Library: pages 27 top left, 32, 33 bottom, 34 top, 34 bottom, 35.
Ag. Franca Speranza: page 62 right.
Sthépane Frances / Hémisphères: pages 57 top right, 59 top left, 93 top left, 81, 104-105, 105 top left.
Robert Frerck / Ag. Franca Speranza: page 120 top left.
Patrick Frilet: page 65 right top.
S. Galeotti / Panda Photo: pages 55 left bottom, 123 right bottom, 130-131.
Alfio Garozzo / White Star Archive: pages 9 top left, 10 top right, 11 top and bottom, 12, 12-13, 13 top left and right, 14 top, 14 center top, 14 center bottom, 14 bottom right, 15, 18-19, 46 left top, 46 right bottom, 46-47, 48 left bottom, 49 top and bottom, 50 top left and right, 51 top and bottom, 52 left bottom, 52-53, 53 top left and right, 57 top left, 58 left center and bottom, 61 top left, 74 left top, 74-75, 76, 77 left top, 77 right top and bottom, 78, 79, 80 left, 80 right bottom, 82, 83, 84 left top and bottom, 84-85, 85 top, 86, 87, 88, 89, 90 top, 90-91, 91 right top, 92 left top and bottom, 93 top right, 94 right top, 98 top left, 99 bottom, 100 left top and center, 101 right, 106, 106-107, 107 top right, 108, 109, 110 top and bottom, 111 top left, 112 center and bottom, 113 bottom, 114-115, 115 bottom left and top right, 116 left, 118, 119, 122 top, 128 top, 136.
L. Giraudou / Regina M. Anzemberger: pages 50-51, 64-65.
L. Giraudon / The Bridgeman Art Library: page 36 bottom.
Michel Gotin / SCOPE: pages 77 left bottom, 114 top left.
A. Greensmith / Ardea London: page 72 top right.
Index, Firenze: pages 26, 30 bottom right, 36 top.
N. Lagrange / Ag. Wallis: page 55 right top.
Charles Lenars: page 130 top.
S. Marmounier / VISA: page 61 top right.
Oliver Martel / Icone: page 122 bottom.
Mastrorillo / SIE: pages 100 top right, 115 bottom right, 125 top.
Molli / Ag. Focus Team: page 80 right top.
J.C. Munoz / PandaPhoto: pages 58-59.
Paolo Negri: page 48 top.
Ernani Orcorte / Realy Easy Star: pages 47 top, 77 left center, 84 right bottom, 92-93.
Christine Osborne/ Alamy Images: page 75 top.
Lara Pessina / Realy Easy Star: page 105 top right.
Photobank: pages 10-11, 60-61, 97 top right, 107 top left, 126-127.
A. Pisard / VISA: page 123 left.
Andrea Pistolesi: pages 55 left top, 62, 62-63, 121 top, 131 top.
Xavier Richer / Ag. Speranza: page 63 right center.
J. Ruiz / VISA: pages 101 left, 103 left top, 128-129.
Anders Ryman /Alamy Images: page 74 bottom.
Scala Archive: pages 23 top left, 44 bottom.
Giovanni Simeone /SIME: pages 3/6, 103 right bottom, 116-117, 121 bottom.
Tauqueur / Ag. Franca Speranza: page 10 top left.
Angelo Tondini / Ag Focus Team: pages 72-73.
Nico Tondini / Ag. Focus: pages 16-17, 114 top right, 126 top.
Yvan Travert / Ag. Speranza: page 60 left top.
T. Valler / VISA: page 99 top.
Sandro Vannini / Ag. Franca Speranza: pages 1, 91 right center, 98 top right, 98-99, 104 center, 110-111, 111 top right, 112-113, 120 top right.
Roger Viollet / Collection Viollet: pages 28 left, 34-35, 39 top, 39 center left, 39 bottom, 41 bottom.
Pawel Wysocki / Ag. Franca Speranza: pages 14 bottom left, 123 bottom.
Pawel Wysocky / Hémisphères: page 58 left top.